WHAT OTHERS ARE SAYING ABOUT THIS BOOK

"The 'How-To' book for being a successful entrepreneur. A must read!"
~ Evan Kosiner, President, *Kosiner Venture Capital*

"I love this book! Beautifully written, engaging and impactful. You will give up your doubt and see how simple succeeding in business can be."
~ Teresa de Grosbois, #1 International Bestselling Author of *Mass Influence*

"Thank you Damian Reid for putting this empowering book together! Anyone who is an entrepreneur or seeks personal development needs to read this book! So many nuggets of wisdom within..."
~ James Erdt, Chief Architect of *WOW* for *DYNAMO Entrepreneur* / Host of *The DYNAMO Show* on Rogers TV, Bestselling Author

"Finally a book that has a cure for the common ailments faced by entrepreneurs! Take two new habits a day and call your banker in the morning!"
~ Odette Laurie, Clarity & Impact Strategist for Entrepreneurs, *Businesswomenontop.com*

"This book is so easy to take action on. You can easily focus on one habit per week and implement those ideas. Damian is easy to relate to and his messages are timeless. As an entrepreneur whose #1 value is FREEDOM this is a fantastic resource."
~ Shanna Landolt, President, *The Landolt Group Recruitment & Executive Search*

"Powerful, perceptive and practical advice with a refreshing scope of perspective that spans all areas of life. This is truly how to live a life you love!"
~ Lesley Edwards, Dating Coach, *Mars Venus Performance Coaching*

"I picked it up and just couldn't put it down. Damian helped transform my business from zero to just shy of six-figures in months, making it easier and less stressful then I ever thought possible. I'm excited to share this book with other entrepreneurs."
~ Bonnie Duarte, The Healing Heart Coach

"This is a brilliant resource for any business owner; if you are looking for code for entrepreneurial freedom then the secrets are right here in this book. As a business owner, I found this to be an easy-to-read resource to help unlock greater potential for success."
~ Natalie Ledwell, Co-Founder of the revolutionary Personal Development company, *Mind Movies LLC*, Motivational Speaker, Bestselling Author and Host of *The Inspiration Show* and *Wake Up TV!*

"Here is a superb resource for any entrepreneur who wants to quickly rise to a whole new level of business and overall life success. A great book."
~ Karen Rowe, #1 International Bestselling Author & Ghostwriter

"This book empowers success at every level! A goldmine of practical advice that makes business simple and helped me harness success in a way I never thought possible. It's the only business book you'll ever need."
~ Kim McLaughlin, Founder, Lyra Communications Corp.

"In 'Cure Entrepreneurialitis', Damian presents several dynamic and poignant habits to increase performance. A remarkable collection of tools to enhance freedom in life!"
~ Robin H-C, Behaviorist and Bestselling Author of *Life's in Session*

"Damian Reid has put together an amazing collection of effective and essential advice for motivated business owners who could benefit from the cure for Entrepreneurialitis."
~ Ken Honda, Bestselling Japanese Author and Speaker

"Damian's book is a helpful and easy-to-read resource that is profound in its scope and its clarity. I believe our habits create our success and this book is loaded with intelligent habits you can implement into your business immediately."
~ Colin Sprake, 4 Times Bestselling Author and 2 Times Quilly Award Winner

Cure

'Entrepreneurialitis'

52 Habits To Earn The
FREEDOM You Deserve

DAMIAN M. REID

Cure 'Entrepreneurialitis'

52 Habits to Earn The FREEDOM You Deserve

Damian M. Reid

Published by: FREEDOM Publishing, a division of Amorvita Inc.,
1 Scott Street, Suite 706, Toronto, Ontario M5E 1A1

First Edition, 2016

Published in Canada

ISBN: **0995247501**
ISBN-13: **978-0995247505 (FREEDOM Publishing)**

FOR MY DAUGHTER KAELEIGH

Your boundless love and passion for life inspire me to greater heights every day. I hope this book inspires you and the next generation of entrepreneurs to embrace living with FREEDOM as a right granted to the courageous.

The Road Not Taken
by Robert Frost

Two roads diverged in a yellow wood,
And sorry I could not travel both
And be one traveler, long I stood
And looked down one as far as I could
To where it bent in the undergrowth;

Then took the other, as just as fair
And having perhaps the better claim,
Because it was grassy and wanted wear;
Though as for that the passing there
Had worn them really about the same,

And both that morning equally lay
In leaves no step had trodden black.
Oh, I kept the first for another day!
Yet knowing how way leads on to way,
I doubted if I should ever come back.

I shall be telling this with a sigh
Somewhere ages and ages hence:
Two roads diverged in a wood, and I —
I took the one less traveled by,
And that has made all the difference.

CONTENTS

Warning—Disclaimer

This book is designed to provide information on living life as a small business owner. It is sold with the understanding that the publisher and author are not engaged in rendering legal, accounting or other professional services. If legal or other expert assistance is required, the services of a competent professional should be sought.

It is not the purpose of this book to reprint all the information that is otherwise available to small business owners, but instead to complement, amplify and supplement other texts. You are urged to read all of the available material, learn as much as possible about running a business, and tailor the information to your individual needs.

Being a small business owner is not a get-rich-quick scheme. Anyone who decides to write and publish a book must expect to invest a lot of time and effort into it. For many people, being a small business owner is more lucrative than working for a company, and many have built solid, growing, rewarding businesses.

Every effort has been made to make this book as complete and as accurate as possible. However, there may be mistakes, both typographical and in content. Therefore, this text should be used only as a general guide and not as the ultimate source of running a small business. Furthermore, this manual contains information that is current only up to the printing date.

The purpose of this manual is to educate and entertain. The author and FREEDOM Publishing shall have neither liability nor responsibility to any person or entity with respect to any loss or damage caused, or alleged to have been caused, directly or indirectly, by the information contained in this book.

If you do not wish to be bound by the above, you may return this book to the publisher for a full refund.

ACKNOWLEDGMENTS

Thank you to the following individuals who without their contributions and support this book would not have been written:

My mom, Barbara Reid, for the gift of my life and providing the first courageous example of being an entrepreneur for me to follow.

My dad, Alan McG. Reid Sr., you showed me the most important path to follow is one where I can live with myself and the choices I make.

My stepmom, Joycelyn Reid, always the voice of love and support.

My siblings, Dominic, Alan Jr. and Alexis Reid and my adopted brother Bryan Duarte, I love you all so much. Thank you for believing in me and my 'crazy' ideas.

My editors Bree Crowder and Joanna Guerriere. Bree, you pulled no punches and called it the way you saw it, thank you! Jo, you have been a friend, confidant, task master, soul partner and my biggest champion through this process. Thank you for turning raw content into something that can make a real difference for entrepreneurs. I love you!

Colin Sprake, Evan Kosiner, James Erdt and Ken Honda for trusting me and agreeing to be the first entrepreneurs interviewed for the book and the podcast series to follow, *Small Business Entrepreneurs Achieving FREEDOM.*

Amy Neiman thank you for cracking the code on my writer's block. Thank goodness for that brainstorming weekend. You are a true miracle!

Nechama Sapirman thank you for being the best friend anyone could ever ask for. You made more contributions to this project than I have room to acknowledge. Big hugs and lots of love!

All the current and past Amorvita Associates, Cynthia Phillip, Michele Hanson O'Reggio, Andrzej Misiak, Lesley Edwards, Beth Ostrander, Bonnie Duarte, Shawn Bearman, Kathleen Day, Kim McLaughlin, Stuart McConnell, Karen Rowe, Michael Santonato, Deborah Knight, Elisa Birnbaum, Gary Montalvo, Jen Mulhall, Jo Caragh, Kay Layne, Maya Mathias, Rod Ward, Stephen de Wit, Tammy Brumwell, Tina Dietz and Wendy Knight Agard. Your unwavering support and confidence has meant the world to me over the last few years! I learn so much from all of you every day. Thank you, thank you, thank you!

Michael Santonato, Karen Toth, Natasha Reid, Mimi Huberman, Sunni VonMutius, Cynthia Phillip, Kim McLaughlin, Nat Harward and Shawn Bearman thank you for the gift of your time to help coax the ideas from inside my head.

The coaches and mentors in my life who contributed to the person I am today - Gail Legacic, Sandy Bernacek, Debbie Wood, Tammy Sturge, Paul Heino, Tony Rumball, Howard Chang, Lesley Edwards, Afrin Khan, David Cunningham, Larry Pearson, Bert Peterson, Jerry Baden, Colin Sprake, Shanna Landolt, Nat Harward, Anna Rosenberg, Bonnie Duarte, Bruce Sloane, Hugh Molyneux, Lynn Giuliani, Ramin Mesgarlou, Alan Cahn, Lior Skaler and Glenn Cooper. I take the best of each of you with me every day to make the difference I am on the planet to fulfill.

My Accountability Partner, Endurance Coach and brah, Nat Harward, thank you for all the moments of support to continue to move forward, especially when I didn't want to. You push me to heights I don't even imagine I can reach all the time! I treasure our relationship.

My partner, Sunni VonMutius thank you for your love, wisdom and opening new doors to me. Life without Kirk O'Connor, Sarah Shaw and Natasha Reid's love would not be the same.

Elizabeth Barlow it would take too many years to try and define and understand our connection. You have opened my soul to miracles and I will forever be thankful and full of love.

Last and certainly not least, all of my clients past, present and future. This book is for you. I honour your courage and thank you for the gift you are to the world. I get to fulfill my *Why* only because you exist. I love you with all my heart.

I have not attempted to cite in the text all the authorities and sources consulted in the preparation of this book. To do so would require more space than is available. The list would include departments of various governments, libraries, industrial institutions, periodicals and many individuals.

PREFACE

What's the difference between an entrepreneur and a small business owner?

The Merriam-Webster dictionary defines an entrepreneur as a person who starts a business and is willing to risk loss in order to make money.[1]

The definition of a small business owner is someone who independently owns and operates a company that is limited in size and in revenue depending on the industry. Someone who owns a local bakery that employs 10 people is an example of a small business owner. Similarly, someone who owns a manufacturing facility that employees less than 500 people is an example of a small business owner.[2]

People often use the terms entrepreneur and small business owner interchangeably. The terms are often used inaccurately and the difference between them is important. While all small business owners are entrepreneurs, not all entrepreneurs are small business owners.

Many entrepreneurs grind out hours and work incredibly hard, yet still don't have, by their standards, successful businesses. And what's more, they certainly don't have the freedom they had visions of when they started their businesses.

In fact, many entrepreneurs can feel like they have even less freedom than they had while they worked for someone else because their entire business now depends on them on a daily basis. Time off means temporarily halting

---

[1] http://www.merriam-webster.com/dictionary/entrepreneur
[2] http://www.yourdictionary.com/small-business

the business. Sometimes it can seem to them as if they just keep working and working and working yet their business does not grow in proportion to their effort.

If this resonates with you at all, this book has found you at the perfect time.

What we have in life is a direct result of our habits. The habits in this book can dramatically transform you, your business and your experience of being an entrepreneur. I'm glad you're here. You're about to find out how to be an entrepreneur with a thriving, successful business and freedom at the same time.

I'm not looking in this book at entrepreneurs like Richard Branson. I'm talking about small business owners and self-employed professionals – those running companies with between 1 to 99 employees. While the practices and habits in this book can apply to *any* business owner, my passion is strongest for micro-enterprises (9 employees or less).

I started my first micro-enterprise in Mom's basement in Toronto at 13 years old. It was a complete accident. I discovered people would pay me to play music I loved. It also allowed me to completely geek out as a DJ on the mixer I built from scratch.

Over the next few years, I grew a team of 7 people to work with me on this. On a regular basis, we beat *MuchMusic* and one of Toronto's top radio station's road shows in popularity. We received the call backs when they didn't. And even though we worked hard, it seemed effortless at the time. Our biggest success factor was that we loved what we were doing!

There have been 5 others since that first business. You could say that following an entrepreneurial path is in my blood. As a third generation business owner, I grew up learning the ins and outs of managing small businesses. I've lived in this world for most of my adult life.

Life was not always laughs and giggles. At 10 years old, my family immigrated to Toronto from Guyana, South America. The happy-go-lucky, bright kid immediately didn't fit in. I dressed funny, had an accent and skipped a grade.

One day, the band teacher got mad and threw a blackboard eraser at me. Then he called me 'woolly' because of my afro. The nickname stuck and I was teased about it all the time. My elementary school memories are full of lonely moments living on the outside looking in.

In early high school, I faced racial discrimination and became suicidal. Life seemed really tough. But I discovered I had one reliable source of joy: Playing music for hundreds while they danced with excitement. I began to look forward to every event I did with my amazing team.

I grew up watching my Mom work on her businesses in the evenings after coming home from her 9 to 5 j-o-b. She was a proud, single mother and worked really hard to provide for my brother and I. I always thought there must be a better alternative to managing on her own and working that hard. After all my team had lots of success and it never felt like hard work. What was our secret sauce?

The habits in this book represent years of research as well as trial and error. I have lived life as an entrepreneur with poor habits; habits that contributed to poor health, bankruptcy, desperation, dissatisfaction and 'burn outs.'

I have also lived in times of bliss, fulfillment and freedom.

I started to notice the difference between the two states. I realized that I have everything to say about whether I am living a life of freedom or not.

I am committed you never have to walk the entrepreneurial journey on your own like my Mom did. Too many entrepreneurs go it alone when it's not necessary. I know personally what feeling alone can do to someone and the deep holes we can dig ourselves into.

I am committed you experience a community full of support and resources. That they personify the wind beneath your wings. Every time I lean back into the support of my family, friends and colleagues I am stronger for it. This book would never exist if not for them.

I have been asked why I chose to write this book. I am not a natural writer. When I first created my bucket list, the first item I wrote down was to write a book. At the time it seemed like nothing more than a grand wish.

Bringing this book from my head to print occurs to me like giving birth to an oversized baby. However, I say that with all possible respect for the mothers in the world – having seen my daughter's birth, I always laugh when a man supposes he can imagine what that's like. No you can't! While I acknowledge this fact, writing this book seems to me to be the closest I could get to experiencing something like that.

The idea for this book arose one day out of anger: Anger at the situation I saw entrepreneurs around me experiencing. Anger at the lack of FREEDOM pervasive in the entrepreneurial world.

Granted, what freedom means to each person is different. For some, freedom means the ability to spend time with their family when they desire, like playing in the park with their young children during a weekday afternoon. For others, freedom is acquiring the finances to travel often or around the world. Or to be able to claim 8 weeks off every year. Or it could be knocking items off the bucket list without having to worry if the bills are paid.

Most importantly, every entrepreneur I meet started their business with a vision that included *some form of freedom*: Freedom of time, money, flexibility, etc. And most are not experiencing that freedom now.

There are many things that contribute to that. Today more and more people are working longer and longer hours while taking home less pay as a value exchange for their work. The world is in the middle of a sleep crisis. We spend less time with our loved ones on average. We babysit our young people and teens with technology.

We dream about discovering more hours in the day to spend on the things we enjoy. We feel embarrassed that we're missing a solution someone else figured out. How do we accomplish more in the time we have?

I truly believe entrepreneurs are the most courageous people on the planet. A fire fighter, while also extremely courageous, may rush into a burning building a couple of times a year. But an entrepreneur wakes up *every single day* to face the unknown. They do it without guaranteed pay cheques, vacations or job security. Worse, they often face the unknown completely alone.

So I was furious the day I decided to write this book. I thought, *Too many of my fellow entrepreneurs are living this way.* I decided in that moment that I could either live as someone who got angry and mouthed off about it, or I could make the kind of difference I was placed on the planet to make. I chose the latter and the condition 'Entrepreneurialitis' was invented.

I define 'Entrepreneurialitis' as a state of existence absent of the FREEDOM intended by an entrepreneur when he/she started his/her business. It is typically characterized by a combination of working longer hours, earning less income, having less vitality and/or spending less time on the important things in life than planned or desired.

I see many not living the life they started their business to experience. When I ask, 'Do you love being an entrepreneur?' or 'Do you love being a small business owner?' Usually people say, 'Yes.' Of course that's also the answer you expect. But when you dig deeper, you find it's not true. You find that they are experiencing some or all of the four conditions outlined in my definition of 'Entrepreneurialitis'.

I recognized that if I wanted to tackle a cure for 'Entrepreneurialitis,' I needed to think differently—outside the norm. The 52 habits were born out of this quest. I share these new ways of thinking with you in each of the habits in this book. Throughout the book I also share why I find the entrepreneurial system today is broken. I examine why traditional coaching and advice contributes to the condition.

One of the main things that I have found contributes to 'Entrpreneurialitis' is the way we organize our work and the rest of our lives. I'm often invited to speak on a topic dear to my heart, 'Why Work:Life Balance is Crap!' Are you ready to shatter your notion of work:life balance? Are you sure? Because after this, you will likely never utter those words again. You will find yourself correcting others.

Let's begin with a 'balance' or weighing device. It consists of a rigid beam horizontally suspended by a low-friction support at its center. It has identical weighing pans hung at either end. One pan holds an unknown weight while the weight in the other is increased by known amounts until the beam is level and motionless.

Work:life balance implies that work is on one side of the weighing device, while life is on the other. This is not how life works.

In reality, there are many area of life that are all equally important. To provide a tool to be able to work with these areas, I created the *Entrepreneur's 12 Key Areas of Life*. We will get into these in detail in Chapter 4, *Love*. One of the 12 Key Areas is *Business*. It includes all the activities you engage in that include your regular occupation, profession, trade or time and attention to acquiring knowledge on an academic subject. In other words, anything you would consider 'work' or learning related to your work or career.

According to the Guinness World Records, the heaviest person in medical history was Jon Brower Minnoch.[3] In March 1978, Jon was admitted to

---

[3] http://www.guinnessworldrecords.com/world-records/heaviest-man

University Hospital, Seattle, weighing more than 635 kg or 1,400 lb. It took a dozen firemen and an improvised stretcher to move him from his home to a ferry-boat. When he arrived at the hospital, he needed two beds pushed together. It took 13 people to roll him over.

Imagine that Jon represents the Key Area of Life *Business* and we seat him on one side of our imaginary balance.

The average human weighs 137 pounds. Let's have each of the remaining 11 Keys Areas of Life be represented by an average person. 11 people x 137 lbs. equals approximately 1,500 pounds.

Let's put those 11 people on the other side of the balance. The balance tips in favour of the 11, as 1,500 lbs. are heavier than 1,400. Eleven Key Areas of Life never balances with one. The biggest, baddest, heaviest area *Business* will never balance with the other 11 Key Areas of Life.

In a 'Work:Life Balance' conversation, you are always looking to find what you can add to or remove from one side of the equation to equal the other. This never produces the result you want. It's a useless exercise.

So if this dual balance is not the answer, what is?

The 12 Key Areas of Life are divided into an internal and external set of 6 Key Areas each. Imagine that each of the 6 *Internal* Key Areas of Life equals 1/6 of a circle. And imagine that each of the 6 *External* Key Areas of Life equals 1/6 of another circle.

Let's take those circles and make them the front and back wheels of a bicycle. What happens when the parts of the wheels exist at different levels? Riding the bicycle becomes difficult and bumpy. But what is it like when each of the pieces of the wheels are at close to the same level? The ride is smoother and easier. If each of the Key Areas equal a level of 6/10 or 8/10 the effect is the same. The ride remains smooth.

Instead of relating to your life and the 12 Key Areas from a context of 'balance,' which brings to mind the two opposing sides of a scale, I invite you to think of your life from a context of *'equilibrium.'* From the perspective of equilibrium your attention equally includes all 12 Key Areas of Life.

Work or *Business* is one of the 12 Key Areas. We want our lives—all 12 areas—to exist in a state of equilibrium. Wouldn't you rather experience *all* of the areas of your life working at the same time? Isn't that preferable over the never-ending struggle to find *'balance?'* The 52 habits in this book exist to support you in your journey towards equilibrium.

Before we jump into the habits, I want to clarify what I mean by the word 'power' as I use it often throughout the book. Power is an overused word – people say it without being conscious of its actual meaning.

The Merriam-Webster dictionary defines power as the ability to act or produce an effect.[4]

Power is the ability to produce a specific result in a specific period of time. Increasing your power means producing *increased results* in the *same* period of time, or producing the same results in a shorter period of time. Power is directly related to *freedom.* The more power you have, the more freedom you have. The 52 habits are designed to give you more power, therefore giving you access to the freedom you want.

And just before we begin, let me take you through a quick walk through the book and its five chapters: *Grow, Organize, Aspire, Love* and *Structure.*

In the first chapter, *Grow,* we'll take a look at how human beings are naturally driven to grow and develop. Doing more of what you love and experiencing freedom requires the growth of self and the ongoing development of your mental, emotional and physiological faculties. These 8 habits develop you into a stronger entrepreneur and a better, evolving you.

In the second chapter, *Organize,* we'll focus on how to be a small business owner who won't waste the precious 168 hours you own every week. We'll create eight practices to free up time to enable you to focus on your genius. You'll gain access to accomplishing more than you can currently conceive possible.

Next we'll dive into the *Aspire* habits that will change the trajectory of your life. If you plan to live with more freedom you will require a compass. You will clarify what everything you're doing is for and where you're going.

In chapter four, *Love,* we explore the *Entrepreneur's 12 Key Areas of Life* and what it takes to earn true equilibrium. What will you need to learn and implement to experience living a life of having it all?

---

[4] http://www.merriam-webster.com/dictionary/power

Our final chapter is *Structure*. These habits will draw the line between good intentions and producing exceptional results. You will learn how to care for the #1 resource in your business and the one often neglected: *You*. You will develop strength, speed, health and smarts.

Taking action is the only way to implement change. These habits will open access to the life of freedom you desire. I'll walk you through how to implement and practice each habit so you can begin making the correct changes in your life today. At the end of this journey together, you will have 52 habits – one new habit for every week of the year. They will have you living an entrepreneurial life with *freedom*.

I recommend you read the book in its entirety before starting implementation. Each habit is about a 4 minute read. You will discover that you've already mastered some. Others will take practice. All 52 habits are listed at the back of the book for easy reference. Don't spoil it and go there now!

I'm not asking you to adopt all 52 habits. I am giving you a one-year challenge. Read the book in entirety, and then take on practicing one new habit every week, for one year. See if you like each habit and if each works for you. Keep whatever works and dump what doesn't.

No one embodies mastery of all of the habits. This book is an opportunity to travel on a fabulous path of discovery and learning. Even if you only adopt *one* new habit from this book you will experience more freedom. The question to ask yourself is, how far along the spectrum of struggle and freedom do you wish to travel? Are you willing to implement the habits required to earn that freedom?

My deep, profound wish for you is that you fulfill the dreams you had imagined when starting your business. That your dreams become reality, *today*. Not sometime in the future when you make more money or experience more time. You deserve that freedom now. It's time to earn it!

Enjoy the book! I am so excited you're on this journey with me. I acknowledge you for your commitment to living the life you desire. I recognize that choosing the entrepreneurial route is not the easiest path through life. And you are the courageous one who chose it anyway. I celebrate your courage!

I am thrilled that you found your way to my book. Things in your life are going are going to be different now. I am so excited for you!

To connect with me and the entrepreneur FREEDOM community visit **entrepreneurialitis.com**. Get access to exclusive interviews with notable entrepreneurs, tools, community resources and lots more.

FREEDOM QUIZ

Is trying to sustain 'balance' (or as I prefer 'equilibrium') in your entrepreneurial life making you feel like you are walking a tightrope? If you answered, 'Hell yes!,' you are not alone. With many demands on our time and energy, we often experience life as a three-ring circus.

In 2012, a Globe and Mail article stated only 23% of Canadians were highly satisfied with life. This was only half as many as were reported in 1991 and there's no sign of improvement on the horizon. Last year, Wall Street's *Bloomberg* published an article titled: *5 Charts That Show Work:Life Balance is Dead.* The article suggested that life balance is steadily becoming a unicorn in the working world.

Take this quick test to discover how well you are living a harmonious and powerful life. Answer each statement 'True' or 'False.' (TIP: The statement is either completely true or it is to be counted as false.)

- I practice taking care of myself first knowing that successfully managing my life requires me to be well physically, emotionally and mentally.
- I exercise regularly, at least 20 minutes 3 times per week.
- I eat healthy meals a minimum of 3 times a day and don't skip breakfast.
- I get physical health check-ups, go to the dentist, and take preventative health precautions.
- I don't feel overwhelmed and have an effective way to keep track of and manage all the things not currently scheduled in my calendar.
- I make personal, quiet time for myself, whether I'm meditating,

reading for pleasure or simply letting my thoughts wander.

- I regularly engage in activities I love to refresh my mind or body that provide enjoyment, stimulation, amusement or pleasure.
- I take regular time off from my work including at least 3 weeks of vacation per year and at least one full day a week where I don't touch work.
- I spend quality time with family and friends enriching my life.
- I feel happy most of the time and regularly experience being content and joyful.
- I contribute my time, energy and experience to achieve or cause things in the world that matter and are important to me.
- I notice and listen to the emotional signals that tell me I'm out of balance. For example: avoidance, irritability, overwhelm, resentment or worry.
- I listen to and honour the requests my body makes for things like a nap, a walk, healthy food, a hug, a massage, etc.
- When I notice I'm beginning to feel unwell, I stop and take the time I need to take care of myself.
- I only schedule meetings that forward my top priorities and have a powerful relationship to saying 'no' to requests for my time. I am able to say 'no' when something doesn't fit with my priorities or goals.
- I have regular date times with my significant other or find time to date if I am single.
- When I have something planned for myself, I don't just toss that aside when someone makes a request of me.
- I have clutter-free environments surrounding me at home and work that promote peace, growth, health, progress and clarity.
- I commit regular time to improve my knowledge, talents and potential that forwards the realization of my dreams and aspirations.
- I have a powerful relationship to my finances and a clear, viable plan to take care of my and my family's needs after I stop working.

Count how many *True* answers you got and compare your count to the ranges below:

16-20 *True*: You are living a **powerful and harmonious life**. Keep up the great work! Where can you make the small changes to elevate yourself to another level? Keep reading to find out!

11-15 *True*: You are **performing better** than many entrepreneurs. Take a moment to acknowledge yourself for the things you are managing correctly.

What new habits that you learn about in the next chapters will increase your experience of freedom and balance?

6-10 *True*: You likely see life from a place of **overwhelm and a lack of balance**. I'm so glad this book found you. It's time to learn new actions and live the life you started your business to enjoy.

0-5 *True*: Stop! This represents an **emergency**. You are headed toward a future where your body and your results will demand changes. Keep reading to get the support you require to make the adjustments you need to make to start earning freedom!

DAMIAN M. REID

CHAPTER **ONE**

GROW

Surround Yourself With Like-Minded People

'Keep away from people who try to belittle your ambitions. Small people always do that, but the really great make you feel that you, too, can become great. When you are seeking to bring big plans to fruition it is important with whom you regularly associate. Hang out with friends who are like-minded and who are also designing purpose-filled lives. Similarly be that kind of a friend for your friends.'
~ Mark Twain, author, *The Adventures of Huckleberry Finn*

Why would I want to surround myself with like-minded people? The whole reason you want to look for like-minded people is that like pulls for like. Let's say you are training for a marathon, as I am for my first. You could surround yourself with a bunch of couch potatoes – people who eat chips, drink beer, play video games, stay up late and don't exercise. That does not pull for early mornings, working out, living a marathon lifestyle, or successfully completing marathons. The same is true of business and being an entrepreneur.

I am not saying to turn over all of your colleagues and friends. Rather, surround yourself with and welcome in new people who will help you achieve your goals. Have your inner circle pulling for what you want in life.

I welcomed a business coach when I was first launching *Amorvita* years ago – one pulling for the kind of lifestyle and freedom I'm committed to. I participated in a high-level, business mastermind program with that coach. The mastermind included entrepreneurs committed to working together and sharing resources for mutual success. During the program, the group travelled to Thailand. We shared an interest in having our businesses create travel as part of our lifestyle.

People in that group included my endurance coach, Nat Harward who is training me for an Ironman competition in a couple of years. Members of the mastermind were not all-work-and-no-play types. Our working retreats were in the Mayan Riviera and Alaska instead of Chicago. We combined work with time for panning for gold and visiting glaciers. Running through the mountains of Juneau for my long run of the week is something I will never forget.

As I got more serious about my training, I noticed I was making small, subtle shifts in who I surrounded myself with. It's important for me to be up early in the morning to do my workouts by 7 AM and be in bed no later than midnight. I started seeing my 'night owl' friends earlier in the day. I stopped taking phone calls after 10:15 PM. I added people to my life who had an interest in having their bodies work at optimum performance levels.

Are you are interested in living a particular kind of life and right now you don't have what you want? If the answer is 'yes,' surround yourself with people that pull in the direction of the kind of life you want. If you want to work fewer hours, don't surround yourself with people who are working 80-hour work weeks. People working 80-hour work weeks will pull you towards 80-hour work weeks.

I often get asked things like, 'What do I do with those relationships?' 'How do I look for like-minded people when my environment is not filled with like-minded people?' 'If I'm already in an environment that doesn't pull for what I want, what do I do to find it? How can I discover it?'

First of all, keep those relationships. They are still business colleagues, acquaintances and people you care about. Simply shift your focus to spending more time with those living the kind of entrepreneurial lifestyle you want.

You might have fears about spending less time with certain people in your life. Sometimes business owners have fears or concerns about letting people go. What if they lose out on something? They ask questions like, 'What if I'm not around those people and I start to become less productive?' 'What's going to happen to my business?' 'Am I going to make enough money?' 'Am I going to work hard enough?' 'Am I going to be at a disadvantage?'

Motivational speaker Jim Rohn said that we are the average of the five people we spend the most time with. One reason people get stuck not making the kind of income they want is that they hang out with people who are also not making money. If you start spending time with people who know how to handle money, you will also learn how to handle money. It just makes sense. Stop hanging out with business owners who can't pay their bills and who complain about money. Those people have little to offer you in having your business be successful.

I am not saying if your brother isn't earning a big income that he should be less important in your life. But there's something to consider if he is living inconsistently with the freedom you want. It's time to look at how much you allow that to pull for the same in your life. You can love someone very much and at the same time choose to subscribe to a different lifestyle. Are you willing to make the difficult choices to stack the deck in your favour?

My life is now filled with people and fellow business owners who align with my values and commitments. I keep those that don't at a relative distance. I never considered myself an endurance athlete until recently. Now I notice clients and others starting to ask my advice about their own fitness and well-being. I love that I have seen myself grow in this area and that I now know experts that I can connect them with to support them as well.

Practice Tips:

- Start by finding one person who is living life in the direction you want and take them to coffee.
- Go slowly. This is not a radical change. You are not going to uproot your entire network all at once, nor should you be striving to.
- Identify people inside your current network living the kind of life you want. Find ways to work side by side with them. For example, co-work together or create joint projects and mastermind groups.
- Notice people near the people in your network who are living the life you want. Reach out to connect with that part of your network.
- Apply this principle to different areas of your life in which you wish to make a difference. It is not limited only to business.

Habit #1: Spend intentional time with business owners who live their dreams and operate the way you aspire to.

Network, Network, Network

'Every person is defined by the communities she belongs to.'
~ Orsen Scott Card, novelist, *Ender's Game*

For nine out of ten entrepreneurs, their business success depends on conversations with others. Few business owners are set up to make lots of money while they sleep. We have all heard wonderful stories about the business miracles: The person whose *YouTube* video went viral and now they are a multimillionaire—now everyone is posting videos hoping theirs does too. Are you posting on social media hoping thousands will flock to your website and buy your services? This is a fantasy for most. People who want to sell you magic courses to have this happen to you feed this delusion.

The truth is, you have to be out there actually having people see you and know you and you have to be speaking about your business. Most people do it or know they should be doing it but don't fully understand *why* they should do it. Why is networking so important?

Consider this:

- It gets you out there in the world and out from the comfortable space you live in.
- You practice speaking about what you offer, your passion and your business.
- Networking environments are less threatening than your live sales conversations.
- You get to practice conversations and work out the details with people other than your strong prospects.
- When you take your new elevator pitch to an event, you can experiment with different ways of talking about your business and see how it goes.

I was recently at a networking event and decided I would try something new. I used to start with a question to pre-qualify the person. I'm always experimenting and testing. I tried something new. The new introduction went something like this…

Are you an entrepreneur? Do you have the life or freedom you imagined when you started your business? Many business owners are working more hours than they want. They're earning less money than they planned. They don't have the energy or time to spend on the things that are important to them. And they're afraid and embarrassed to let anyone know their real situation. My name is Damian Reid and I have a 7-step system to eliminate this situation in your business and your life. I have people do more of what they love to do.

When I said that, people said, 'Whoa, that sounds really cool! What do you do?' Instead of me pitching them, my opening actually had them ask me questions and engage in what I was all about. I connected with more people. They were interested. I received more qualified business cards than at any other event. You bet I was showing up as memorable for them vs. others who were saying, 'I'm a lawyer,' 'I'm a coach,' 'I'm a real estate agent,' etc.

Recent *HubSpot* statistics show the importance of networking and being face-to-face with business colleagues. 85% of those surveyed say they build stronger, more meaningful business relationships during in-person business meetings and conferences. 77% say they prefer in-person meetings due to the ability to read body language and facial expressions. Finally, 49% say they prefer in-person business meetings because they allow for more complex strategic thinking.[5]

Every week, attend at least one group networking event and a one-on-one meeting. Group networking can include events like *BNI* type, chamber of commerce and *Meetup* events, for example. Do your homework. Some will be better and more appropriate than others. If you take 4 weeks of vacation, you will attend at least 48 group networking events in a year.

One-on-ones are also important. I reserve these for people I have prequalified and who there is a strong chance of a partnership with. There is something about face-to-face conversations that's valuable in creating relationships. I like to do coffee or hot chocolate in my case. Sometimes it's virtual hot chocolate using *Skype*, *Zoom* or *FaceTime*. I schedule an hour if it's a live meeting and 15 minutes if virtual. If we finish faster, I just found time to work on other activities. We are both busy entrepreneurs happy to have spent time together.

As you practice this, you will learn more about yourself and who you want to surround yourself with. You will start to refine your likes and dislikes. Networking supports Habit #1. You start to see the types of people and vibes you want to add into your circle of influence and the types you don't.

Networking has you step outside your comfort zone. People are generally

---

[5] blog.hubspot.com/sales/face-to-face-networking-stats

uncomfortable speaking in public. It puts you in an unfamiliar situation with people you don't know and forces you to interact. Most don't know I am fairly introverted. People see me in public or at the front of a room and think I like being in the spotlight. EVERY time I go to an event or walk up to the front of a room I'm speaking in, my body functions do all sorts of weird things. I am a nervous wreck for the first few minutes until I can relax and start making a difference with whoever I'm talking to.

If you feel uncomfortable at networking events, try pushing yourself to do more public speaking. The more often you push beyond your fear of speaking at the front of a room the more easily you'll push past your fear of speaking to anyone.

Not long ago, my coach surprised me and asked me to demonstrate to a group how to hold and command 'the space of a room.' After I spoke, someone said, 'Isn't it amazing that Damian is so comfortable up there?!' I explained that the whole time my knees were shaking and my stomach was in knots. I said, 'I'm not comfortable at all but you don't see it.'

Public speaking increases the ease with yourself and your business. The biggest difference it's made for me is in getting comfortable with people faster. I have less than a minute with my elevator pitch.

I had better get comfortable right away or it's over and I am still uncomfortable. The more you get out there and talk to people, the faster you will become comfortable doing it.

Pick networking events that are a match for what you love and have fun. If you like wine, go to a wine event. If you like the outdoors or water find events in the summer on a boat. It doesn't have to be the same old 7:30 AM every week in a boardroom. Have it be part of your lifestyle. Also, try events that you wouldn't normally consider and stretch your limits.

You can try joining a group that meets once per month and one of your 4 weeks is handled. The second week pick something that is aligned with what you love. The third week, choose something you wouldn't typically do and try that. For the fourth week, spin the wheel and see what randomly comes up. You want to make sure you have some fun with it.

Remember, the most important thing about networking is that it gets you out. It's scary how many entrepreneurs I encounter that work from their home who rarely get out and interact. Go play with other people. Have an appropriate pitch ready for social occasions. When you are out, be sure to let people know how they can connect with you or assist you. For example, 'I have an event soon and I am interested in having entrepreneurs attend. Who should I talk to?' Or, 'I'm hosting a summit and need speakers to make a difference with entrepreneurs.' Include a call to action or what's the point? Why are you talking to these people? The person you're speaking with might be a perfect fit for you. Or, they may know someone who would be perfect for you to speak to to solve a problem you have, or to forward the intention and reach of your business.

Start networking more. Connecting with people is a huge access to growth and freedom in your business!

Practice Tips:

- Schedule time to prepare event-specific and appropriate networking introductions.
- Include time in your calendar within 24 hours of the event to follow-up with all the connections you made.
- Attend social events like book clubs, charity galas, movie premieres, etc. They are all group networking events. If there's a group of people, it counts!
- Always tell people how they can engage with you.
- When you notice you're getting comfortable find an event that pushes your personal limits. Keep pushing yourself out of your comfort zone.

Habit #2: Attend at least four group networking events and four one-on-ones per month.

Your Biggest Champions

'Coaching is a profession of love. You can't coach people unless you love them.'
~ Eddie Robinson, American football coach (recognized by many college football experts as one of the greatest coaches in history)

Have you ever stopped to wonder why Olympic athletes have coaches? You could answer with something like of course they have coaches, duh! But I want you to really consider the question. Here is this extremely talented athlete. Why do they need a coach? Why not just go out there and perform? I often ask my clients to consider the relationship between Olympic coach and their athlete.

Consider Usain Bolt, regarded as the fastest person ever timed. He is the reigning Olympic champion and world record holder in the 100m, 200m and 4×100m relay. He is the first man at the modern Olympic Games to win six gold medals in sprinting – the first to achieve the 'triple triple', winning the 100m, 200m and 4x100m relay titles at 3 consecutive Olympic Games. He is a pinnacle example of performance. Usain's Coach, Glen Mills, has worked with him since 2004 to produce stunning results.

On your entrepreneurial journey, it's important to have the right support in your corner. That means coaches or programs that can have you be the highest performing entrepreneur possible.

The average competitive sprinter trains about 20 hours a week just to improve by seconds in a race. The coach's job is to take those 20 hours and use them effectively to produce the fastest time possible. Do you relate to yourself as an Olympic athlete in your business?

And it's not just about whether or not you have a coach; it's about *the way you work with your coach*. Another, very important question to ask yourself is this: Are your biggest champions having to work harder than you to increase your performance?

Do you think that Usain's coach goes to his house in the morning, wakes him up and drags him to the track? When his coach says to do his conditioning run or weight training, do you think he argues or refuses? Every minute of every hour of coaching counts. There is no time to waste. Don't put your coach in the position of having to come to your house to wake you.

In my experience, there is no one coach who is right for everybody. Just like every athlete needs the right fit to work with a coach, so do you as an entrepreneur. I once worked with a coach who recommended making sales calls seven days a week. I believe entrepreneurs should take at least one full day off per week (we will get to that in a later habit). Clearly that is not a fit. Later other value differences showed up and we ended the coaching relationship.

Lately, I have been interviewing candidates for my next business coach. The leading candidate said, 'I don't work for you. I work for your vision and the people in future you will make a difference with.' I immediately sat straighter in my chair and paid closer attention. This was a man focused on what matters to me and is aligned with my values.

It's easy as an entrepreneur to understand the importance of a *business* coach. But what about for other areas of your life? My perspective on this is simple and straightforward: When you have an area in your life that you want to achieve freedom, hire the appropriate coach for that area. Sometimes coaches may not have the word 'coach' in their title. The important thing is that someone is in your corner as you biggest champion.

Last year, I worked with stylist, endurance, business, health and relationship coaches. When I ended my engagement years ago, I worked with a divorce and separation coach. Without exception, the results I achieved working with each of these coaches were extraordinary – far beyond anything I could have expected if doing it all on my own.

Bonnie Duarte is a member of the *Amorvita* team and also the coach I worked with during my breakup. She was right there beside me and I moved through the spaces of grief and loss with her. I had my moments where I was upset and just needed a good cry. I went through my angry phase, my blame phase and all the stages of grief. But with her, it was ok to feel what I felt. I had all the room to be myself dealing with a loss. Without her, I would have seen myself as weak and taken longer to heal.

Working with different coaches has opened my eyes to things I never considered. My stylist shrunk my closet by a third and I discovered that 'active wear' has no place at the grocery store! My health coach Anna Rosenberg introduced me to the world of macrobiotics. She was instrumental in me achieving a body that my endurance coach Nat Harward could go to work on.

I don't believe in measuring body weight without a context of health. Anyone can lose weight in an unhealthy way. I was at my heaviest weight just over a year ago. Now I weigh the same as I did when I was half this age and trained 18 hours a week in the martial arts. Now that's an accomplishment! Especially when I have never considered myself an endurance athlete and I am training for an Ironman. I didn't get here alone.

The bottom line is that coaches get you where you want to go faster and better than you can do on your own.

Practice Tips:

- No 'coach stacking.' Pick one coach to work with you in each area of focus. You might find a coach who isn't a fit for you and the overall effectiveness of the coaching in all areas is reduced.

- Choose coaches who have demonstrated that they can produce the results you want. Interview past clients.
- When it's time to say goodbye make the choice without guilt. A coach that can get you to a 5-figure business may not be the one to take you to a 6-figure business.
- Never, never, never stay in a coaching relationship that is not a match for your values.
- Be a responsible adult with your coach. You asked to be coached. Don't turn your coach into an overpaid babysitter. Be Olympic calibre.

Habit #3: Choose an expert coach for every area of your life in which you want to produce extraordinary results.

Immersive Personal Growth

'Whatever the mind can conceive and believe, the mind can achieve.'
~ Dr. Napoleon Hill, author, *Think and Grow Rich*

We live in a society where people are seen to have a higher value when they know more than the average person. Those who know more are able to contribute more than the average person in their field. They tend to be paid higher than the average. Brian Tracy said, 'To earn more, you must learn more.' Achieving freedom and ongoing, positive, personal growth go hand in hand. There are many different types personal growth activities that entrepreneurs can engage in.

This habit does not address daily activities like meditation, spiritual practices, journaling or breathing techniques. We'll look at these and their related habits later in the book. We'll also look a little later at activities specifically related to learning about your business and industry. This will get addressed in Habit #8.

So what is immersive personal growth? We will define it here as personal growth activities that need longer time commitments. While they may support your business as well (as we will go into more detail in in Habit #8), they also address many different key areas of life. Ontological programs offered by *Landmark Worldwide*, Tony Robbins, etc., are examples of immersive personal growth. These are transformative, multi-day programs. This kind of growth can also include activities like tantra workshops, Vipassana (silent retreats) and yoga retreats. Immersive personal growth typically takes place in a group setting versus solo activities.

I recommend entrepreneurs schedule one immersive personal growth activity per quarter. That usually looks like scheduling a multi-day event every three months. Last quarter, a multi-mentor event transformed my thinking in many different areas of life. This quarter, I plan to attend a 3-day financial investment event. It promises to double the current rates of return on my investment portfolio. Next quarter I am considering a 10-day Vipassana silent retreat.

Taking the time to pause and spend a weekend at a yoga retreat or take a few days to do a transformational program is important for our personal growth and development. Immersive personal growth activities provide many benefits in the life of an entrepreneur:

- They create a restorative mental and physical break from day-to-day routine, stresses and challenges.
- They represent a commitment to hit pause and do deeper work not available to us through shorter activities.
- They are an opportunity to create, build and nurture new relationships and communities.
- They allow you to find people to surround yourself with who are living the kind of life you are committed to living.
- They enable you to discover non-business owners who are practicing the types of habits that will make a difference in other areas of life.

Most entrepreneurs will not carve out time for these types of activities. They get completely immersed in their business and don't look up for days and days at a time. The idea of taking time for these activities gets quickly relegated to the back burner, or worse, put on the 'I'll get around to it later when I have more time' list.

This is symptomatic of the same mindset that has so many business owners take little or no vacation time. In North America, most employees receive 10 days of paid vacation per year after a year of service. In the United Kingdom, it's 28 days. Many entrepreneurs I meet started their businesses to increase freedom related to time. Yet, so many of us don't give ourselves the equal time off we would receive if we went to work for someone else.

Many don't take the time to develop themselves through immersive personal growth activities. Available time for these activities will not just appear in your calendar. It takes deliberate effort and planning on your part. It starts with considering the areas you have an interest in developing. Then you must do the necessary planning in your calendar and business operations to enable them to happen.

I have considered the Vipassana 10-day silent meditation retreat for more than a year. Courses at the closest centre to me usually fill up a few months out. Ten days away from my business creates challenges; no access to a phone, the internet or the outside world requires advance planning with my team. Someone has to manage the business and take care of the issues that may arise. Taking this time off means arranging for the care of my private clients and the leading of any courses or programs I am involved in. In my case, this particular activity needs to be planned two to four quarters away.

Implementing this habit is a real opportunity to earn freedom in your business. If you currently do a couple of these activities a year, what would it take to do one per quarter? If you already do one per quarter, what would you need to create to add week-long retreats? Or to make a commitment to spend 7-10 hours per week in a long-term immersive personal growth activity?

Anyone who has ever participated in immersive personal growth activities raves about the value. The story is often the same: It starts out with them saying they could never have imagined how they could take the time off, and ends with them being thankful that they did and looking forward to the next one.

Immersive growth activities serve a dual purpose: First of all, they give us access to achieving entrepreneurial freedom by increasing our knowledge and skills. They also serve as an immediate access to freedom by enabling us to take longer chunks of time away from our day-to-day tasks to work on ourselves and come back refreshed.

Practice Tips:

- Plan well in advance. I would recommend picking your immersive personal growth activities a year in advance. Always have your next four activities chosen.
- Start planning each event with your team and support resources 3-6 months out.
- Pick activities to make the biggest difference in areas you are

struggling with. For example, a Tony Robbins program for motivation, etc.

- Keep expanding your limits. If you currently do two activities, start doing four. If you currently do four weekends, try two weekends and two full weeks, etc.
- Match your choices with the communities you want to build in your life.

Habit #4: Take part in at least one immersive personal growth activity per quarter.

Know Your Trigger Behaviours

'History is a vast early warning system.'
~ Norman Cousins, political journalist, author, professor and world peace advocate

When I say 'trigger behaviours' people usually think about things that create a negative reaction. For example, a client recently said to me that conversations about pharmacology versus alternative health methods are a huge 'trigger' for her. This is not what I am referring to here. There are certain consistent things we do when we get off track and head down the proverbial rabbit hole. I call these things 'trigger behaviours'.

I created this particular habit out of a process of self-education. As much as I would love to say I learned it in a pleasant way, that wasn't the case. I discovered it at one of the lowest points of my life. My business was not making enough money to pay the bills. I was wondering if I should quit and find a job. And I doubted myself and my abilities more than I ever had.

My coach noticed that there were certain things I did when I was confronted and in a downward spiral. I sat down, made a list and ended up with 25 'trigger behaviours.' Then I said, 'I wonder what would happen if I took on a practice of looking at those behaviours once or twice a week?' I chose twice a week because I felt like going a whole week without checking in with myself would be too long.

How this practice works is I pose each of the trigger behaviours as a question. When the answer is 'yes,' this tells me that a trigger behaviour is active. A 'no' indicates a trigger behaviour is *not* active. I'll share 10 out of the 25 on my list with you so that you get a sense of what this practice looks like:

Each trigger behaviour question starts with 'Am I...'

- ... skipping my workouts?
- ... craving or eating shitty food? (I use the actual language of how I say it to myself)
- ... dealing with any symptoms of illness?
- ... craving sex? (people usually laugh and raise their eyebrows at this one. Of course it's normal to have sexual desires. I know for myself when I ask this it's more like a desperate NEED rather than a healthy relationship with sex)
- ... watching *Netflix* or movies during the workday?
- ... avoiding talking to my mother?
- ... worried about money and not in action?
- ... feeling ugly?
- ... being snappy or short with anyone?
- ... no longer 'The One' (to make a difference in how entrepreneurs live with FREEDOM)?

These are all trigger behaviours for me. My practice is to review the list two times a week and send my score to my accountability partner.

I use a scale from *Not Triggered* (0-2 'yes's') all the way to a *High Trigger Zone* (9-11 'yes's'). I can say I'm not triggered if the amount of 'yes's' to the questions is between 0 and 2. It's like an early warning system for me. Sometimes I'm not aware of a specific issue until I get into a conversation with my coach. Then I can spot the issue before I head into a downward spiral. When I need support, I make requests of my accountability partner and support team.

Consider what would be possible if you were to adopt this habit for yourself. An early warning system gives you an opportunity to be pre-emptive. You can examine what you might be avoiding or procrastinating on.

You already know the kind of things that take you off the court or out of the game. For some it's just sitting around and doing nothing. It's like they're frozen and not in action. Other times, other trigger behaviours come up first that *then* result in sitting around and doing nothing. Either way, it's good to know and consistently review what your trigger behaviours are for yourself so you can stay on track.

I discovered the *Netflix* trigger behaviour when working from home. I would grab some lunch and just plan to watch *part* of an episode while eating. Sitting up and eating would turn into slouching back on the couch. Slouching would turn into getting a more comfortable with a cushion behind my head. Then of course the episode finishes and then 20 seconds later, another episode starts. The next thing I know I've watched 2 or 3 episodes all on my 'lunch break' which now has turned into 3 hours!

Everyone has their own trigger behaviours that are unique to them. Knowing what yours are and scheduling a regular time to check-in with yourself is invaluable. Doing it once or twice a week gives you access to getting in front of what might normally take you off track.

Two thoughts cannot occupy the same space at the same time. You cannot think of being free and being confronted by something at the same time. Try it—it's too hard. This habit enables you to stop concentrating on what you're being confronted by and whatever is taking you down the rabbit hole. Identifying a trigger behavior enables you to instead start concentrating on freedom and the 'freedom thoughts' will displace the 'confronted thoughts.'

Sometimes our access to freedom begins with clearing away all the things that get in the way of it. Clear away your trigger behaviours!

Practice Tips:

- When making your trigger behaviour list, trust yourself and don't overthink. Keep your list flexible and add or take away from it when you notice behaviour changes.
- Always have an accountability partner to send your list to. Don't list alone!
- Keep your list electronically in a note or in a *Pages* or *Word* document. It makes it easy to update and forward to your accountability partner.
- Review your 'trigger behaviour' list twice per week until you are reliably and consistently reaching no high trigger zones.
- To get support when you're in a trigger behaviour, speak with an outside source (your coach or an accountability partner for example), or go inward and spend some quality solo time to help you find clarity and direction again. The next habit will help with the latter!

Habit #5: Create a trigger behaviour checklist and review it at least once weekly.

Time With You

'What lies behind us and what lies before us and tiny matters compared to what lies within us.'
~ Ralph Waldo Emerson, essayist, lecturer and poet

This habit is closely related to the last habit: Knowing your trigger behaviours. You now know how to anticipate and prevent a spiral descent into the rabbit hole of negativity and non-productivity. As I mentioned above, to help you get out of a trigger behavior you can choose to get outside support or engage in solo activities to get yourself grounded and focused again. This habit is about the latter.

Recall also in Habit #4 we talked about longer immersive personal growth activities. In this habit, we are also looking at activities that provide valuable and important time with YOU. These activities nourish your mind, body and spirit. But they are different than immersive personal growth activities in that they take *less* time to complete. You can do one or even several in a day. And they are very powerful in giving you access to the freedom to feel great and refresh your mind, body and spirit whenever you need to.

I have time scheduled in my calendar every day for meditation. I use a technique I learned when I was around 12-13 years old and participated in a gifted program. I am now so grateful for having had that teacher and for the lifetime gift she gave me. She taught me a yoga technique that enables me to quickly relax and release any points of tension, anxiety or stress. Sometimes the tension is located in my chest and my breathing feels constricted. Often I feel it in my stomach. It's interesting because sometimes I can relax everything else but can still feel an energy blockage that won't let go until I meditate.

I don't always immediately recognize when I'm dealing with anxiety. When I work at a high pace for a long period of time, the tension stored in my body becomes normal. It begins to show up as different physical symptoms. Sometimes I have trouble sleeping. There can be a tightness in my shoulders and neck that can create headaches. I can have cravings that are on the trigger behaviour list like pizza, junk food and ginger ale. Taking time on my own to meditate enables me to recognize and release the trigger behaviours, and to release anxiety I may not even have known I had.

Taking daily time for activities like meditation, journaling and spiritual practice are important for self-reflection. These activities give us time in our day to pause and reset. If we don't stop to get in touch with our bodies, our spirit and our mind, we miss out on the numerous benefits of doing so. These benefits include increases in focus, energy and a sense of purpose. Because we miss out on these benefits, we experience a decrease in freedom as entrepreneurs in our day-to-day life.

The biggest obstacle for entrepreneurs in implementing this habit is making it a priority. When the day's emergencies start to occur these daily practices are fast to go out the window. At first, they get postponed until later in the day. As time appears to become scarce the plans are cancelled. Often this is rationalized with the thought that we're only missing one day and that there's no harm in doing that.

Deepak Chopra recently said that meditation is one of the best tools we have to counter the brain's negativity bias, release accumulated stress, foster positive experiences and intentions and enjoy the peace of present moment awareness.[6] A large body of research has established that having a regular meditation practice produces tangible benefits for mental and physical health, including[6]:

- Decreased blood pressure and hypertension
- Lowered cholesterol levels
- Reduced production of 'stress hormones' including cortisol and adrenaline
- More efficient oxygen use by the body
- Increased production of the anti-aging hormone DHEA
- Improved immune function
- Decreased anxiety, depression, and insomnia

On days that I miss my midday meditation, my afternoons go very differently. A 10-15 minute meditation in the middle of the day has me feel as fresh as I am after my morning workout and just about to start my day.

Time for these practices will not happen without scheduling the time for them in your calendar. You need to schedule them the same way you need to schedule the immersive personal growth activities in Habit #4. They

---

[6] deepakchopra.com/blog/article/4701

won't just happen if you wait to do them when you feel like doing them or need to.

This doesn't mean that you should restrict yourself to only doing them at the times you schedule them in. Sometimes I notice I'm aggravated. I may be short or snarky with my team. That's a sure sign that it is time for a little me time and an impromptu meditation session is in order. Once that's done I am in a great position to make an apology for my asinine behaviour.

Meditation brings us back to the present moment and it grounds us. There are many different meditation techniques out there for you to explore. To start, close your eyes and notice what's happening with your breath. Just focus on your breath – that's it. By paying attention to your breathing you can tell if you're breathing short or shallow. You can also tell if you are forcing deep breaths to come in and go out or trying to control your breathing. Consider that how you breathe is how you operate in your life.

During meditation, we focus on the breath because it's involuntary. Your body just has to do it. For almost everything else, *you* control if your body does it or not. Breath is the one thing you can focus on that enables you to become present and get your mind to come into the moment.

Sometimes focusing is a real challenge. You can hear yourself saying things like, *I don't have time to do this...when is that alarm going to go off...I know I said 10 minutes but I don't have 10 mins...* If you hear yourself saying things like this, it's an opportunity to notice, pull your focus back to your breath and become present in the moment.

In addition to meditation, I have time scheduled in my calendar to journal at the end of the day. Different people have different journal practices. Choose whatever practice works best for you. If you find yourself without a physical journal you can write in an app on your smartphone. Use your journaling space as a place for random thoughts that are just random thoughts. You can go back and review what you wrote in the last week or last month to notice patterns. It can be an opportunity to catch and follow-up on things that you may have thought were complete but you notice it's become evident that they're not.

You will know if something is complete for you when there is nothing left to do with that item. There is no further action required and no one left for you to communicate with about that item.

Not too long ago my trigger behaviour checklist identified that I was in the

Medium Trigger Zone. At the time I had no idea what was going on. Later that day it landed on me like a tonne of bricks – I had skipped all of my daily practices for the last 3 days. Missing that time with myself left me frazzled, short tempered and stressed. I messaged my accountability partners right away and shared with them what I discovered. I promised to resume my practices right away.

The last area I want to briefly touch on in this habit is spiritual practices, whatever your expression of spirituality is. Part of spending meaningful time with yourself is engaging in spiritual practices that are meaningful to you. We are not going to go deeper into this topic now – In Chapter 4 we will create a habit in the area of Spirituality as one of the *Entrepreneur's 12 Key Areas of Life*. For now, it's simply important to know that engaging in spiritual practices, however they look for you, is important. Scheduling time for them will contribute to the freedom you will experience by spending meaningful time with *you*.

Practice Tips:

- Schedule time in the middle of the day to do a spiritual, meditation and / or journaling practice. Your afternoons will thank you.
- End your day with a journaling practice. Use the opportunity to empty your mind of all of the thoughts that could create restless sleep.
- Schedule time in your calendar for all your 'time with you' practices.
- Remain flexible. Sometimes you need time that isn't scheduled or the time scheduled would be better moved to later.
- Don't skip your daily practices.

Habit #6: Schedule time to spend with yourself and your thoughts…get to know the person within.

Learn More About The Sandbox You Play In

'Entrepreneurship is neither a science nor an art. It is a practice.'
~ Peter Drucker, management consultant, educator and author

What kind of resources are you using to keep you finger on the pulse of what's happening in your industry? It's hard to argue with the need for entrepreneurs to keep on top of the industry sandbox we play in. Yet I notice a lot of entrepreneurs get self-absorbed and stop doing this.

My good friend Natasha works as a producer in the entertainment industry in New York. We talked recently about how the musicians and singers she works with often don't view themselves as entrepreneurs. This presents her with challenges when working with them to increase their success.

Sometimes she gets so micro-task focused she can miss industry events that are important to her and her clients. But by not going to events, she could miss the new group of people coming into the industry who *do* get that they are entrepreneurs. These are potential allies in making the difference she is committed to in the industry. But she can miss them if she is focused on doing everything by herself and has her head down.

As an entrepreneur, it is important for Natasha to keep tuned in and connected to other people in her industry. She has noticed that both the younger and older generations bring different perspectives that are both of value. When she connects with those resources, she often comes back with a fresh perspective. Sometimes a particular marketing approach that someone shares with her at an event is more effective than one she was previously using. She finds new ideas she would never discover if she stayed hunkered down in her bunker.

We covered the value of other sources of information in service of personal growth in Habits #2 (Networking Events), #3 (Coaches) and #4 (Immersive Personal Growth Activities). There is no shortage of knowledge in today's digital age to keep you tapped into your industry. You can subscribe to industry newsletters and updates. You can listen to industry related podcasts. Let's not forget the value of trade specific events and conferences.

It's highly likely that entrepreneurs will get completely absorbed in the day-to-day tasks of running their business. They stop paying attention to what's out there, what's trending and what's in the news. It's easy to forget that we live inside a group of people who run the same kind of businesses.

You need to carve out time every day to research, read, listen to or learn something industry-related. Warren Buffet dedicates 80% of his day to reading. He's not alone. Bill Gates reads about 1 book per week. Elan Musk is an avid reader and when asked how he learned to build rockets, he said, 'I read books.' Oprah Winfrey selects her favourite books every month for her book club to read and discuss.

One challenge we all face is how to sort through all the possible information we could consume. There's just so much out there. How do we choose what's most relevant? One option is to go with the popular vote. You could listen to the entrepreneurial podcasts that rank highest in *iTunes*. You could read the most popular blogs, subscribe to the popular newsletters, etc.

You can also seek out people in your industry who are doing similar things. I know of a fellow author and expert who also focuses on entrepreneurs having freedom. He's from New Zealand and I happened to discover him one day on a telesummit. Most of his tribe is on the other side of the world. I immediately started following him in social media and subscribed to his newsletter. I constantly learn from what he does and can see things I want to adopt and put my own spin on. I also have the opportunity to see practices that don't work for me and my tribe.

It's also important to have a wide range of people you follow in your industry. For example, in my industry, the icons are generally older male speakers. Leaders with household names like Brian Tracy and Tony Robbins have been around for a long time. Some of them like Jim Rohn have passed away but their work still continues to influence and sell. If I only focused on them I would miss the grassroots explosion happening amongst the Millennials and Gen Z's.

Many of those in the younger generations are not following 'traditional,' large scale, online marketing campaign models. They are creating really powerful communities, exchanging information, teaching each other and super-niching. If I miss following their work as well, I could miss the opportunity to gain allies, learn new things and forward my commitments even further.

Going back to Natasha – she's all about social media as her primary source of industry information. She is all over *Twitter*, *Facebook*, *Vine*, *Snapchat*, *YouTube* and whatever's hot and new. She observes people in her industry and how they are using social media. She now also finds events to attend that are industry relevant.

She was sharing with me about a cool, tech event that she found recently. You might think tech and music have nothing to do with each other. I didn't get the connection at first either until she asked me, 'Where do you find your music now?' It's true that these days we find our music online. The event was amazing for Natasha. She was super stoked, met great people and learned a lot. Best of all her ticket was completely free – all because she was keeping up to date on what's happening in her industry.

I schedule one hour every day to do industry-related learning. My sources vary and include newsletter subscriptions, *LinkedIn* groups, social media and podcasts. Sometimes I read the business section of the newspaper for the top news on small businesses. There are lots of reporters creating content. It's waste to leave that on the table. They went out, interviewed people, did the research and summarized it in concise, great articles. Read them!

Practice Tips:

- Do research to learn the best sources of information specific to your industry. Start following or subscribing to them.
- Pick a minimum amount of time you will dedicate every day to learning about your industry. Make that time non-negotiable like brushing your teeth.
- Every 6 months increase your daily time spent on industry learning by at least 15 mins per day.
- Read one expert book from a non-related industry for every 10 books you read from your industry. Processes are transferrable. Start learning how to integrate best practices from other industries into your business.
- Identify 3-5 leading experts in your industry and learn from them.

Habit #7: Read or listen to something industry related every day.

Become A Sales and Marketing Ninja

'It doesn't matter how many times you fail. It doesn't matter how many times you almost get it right. No one is going to know or care about your failures, and neither should you. All you have to do is learn from them and those around you because all that matters in business is that you get it right once. Then everyone can tell you how lucky you are.'
~ Mark Cuban, owner of the NBA's *Dallas Mavericks, Landmark Theatres* and *Magnolia Pictures*

The mythical ninjas are said to have been masters of ingenuity and adaptation. Sales and marketing go hand-in-hand with becoming an entrepreneur who wants to achieve freedom. If you don't take daily actions in this area the freedom you seek is unlikely. You want to take on the mission of becoming a marketing and sales ninja in your business.

Most people collapse marketing and sales. Or, they get confused about the difference. In its simplest form, marketing is about getting known. Sales is about getting purchased. So marketing has people *find* you, and sales has people *pay* you.

Where do you go for marketing and sales advice? There is no shortage of 'experts' who say they can dramatically increase your results. They promise to train you to be able to attract more people to find about what you offer and ultimately buy more from you. I'm always wary of any quick fix solution. At the end of the day it all comes down to a cost vs. return equation. There is always a cost for marketing and sales activities. The question is, how effective are they at actually bringing you a return? And how can you know in advance if this will happen?

I recently attended a workshop with a top Facebook marketer in my industry. He ran us through the psychology and steps for a real life *Facebook* ad optimization sequence. This sequence has been proven to generate consistent revenue for a well-known coaching brand.

He shared the metrics, or as I like to call it, the 'sales math' of the campaign with us. In this campaign, it cost between $6 and $8 to have someone register for a webinar. That's about the norm in this industry. Once the person who registers attends the webinar they receive a product offer and have the option to buy.

When people say things like, 'I run $100,000 worth of Facebook ads,' it's interesting to me. My immediate thought is, *That's nice! What does $100,000 of Facebook ads actually produce for your business?*

Let's do the sales math on $100,000 worth of *Facebook* ads using the high end of the $6-8 range noted above:

- $100,000 of *Facebook* ads at $8 per webinar = 12,500 leads or people registered
- Of the 12,500 registered for the webinar about 40% at the high end will show up = 5,000 attend the webinar
- Of the 5,000 that attend you are able to convert 10% of them = 500 sales
- You need to sell your product for $200 x 500 sales = $100,000 *just to break even* with your advertising spend

Many people don't understand how to calculate their sales math. Part of taking actions to become a better sales and marketing ninja is planning this out. You have got to be able to understand the numbers. It's all simple math and ratios.

You want to consult really great sources of this information and follow strong business practices. Hire a great business coach. Read material to educate yourself so that you have practices that work in your business. Track results and make adjustments to optimize your marketing and sales efforts.

Here's another example of sales math that highlights something for you to consider when selling your service. It's based on some work I recently did with a participant at a mastermind program I was asked to speak at. He delivers a 6-day training program that sells for $1,500. I immediately red-flagged the price point, but that's a discussion for another time. I asked him how many people he wanted to have start the next program. He said 20:

- 20 participants in the program at $1,500 is $30,000 in revenue (his goal)
- He said it takes about 30 conversations right now for every registration. 20 sales x 30 conversations = 600 conversations
- He has 12 weeks to sell the program. 600 conversations / 12 weeks = 50 conversations per week or 10 conversations per day
- He currently has a database of 1,000 prospects
- If he assumes he can reach half those prospects (often it is less than 50%) he has access to only 500 of the 600 conversations needed
- We know that he needs to find leads for another 100 conversations to reach the 600 needed

There are a lot of different places he could impact the effectiveness of his sales efforts. He could work with a coach to have his conversations be more effective. If he only needed 10 conversations for every sale he would need a total of 200 conversations rather than 600. If the program is underpriced and he raises it to $3,000 he would only need 10 sales to make the same amount of money. There are many ways to change his equations, which would all influence his business practices and therefore maximize his resources and time freedom. It's amazing how many business owners operate their businesses without understanding their basic sales math.

In my experience, many entrepreneurs get a glazed-eyed look when the topic of sales comes up. There are certainly not many screaming, 'Yahoo! I can't wait to get started!' Instead, they avoid talking about it. They do anything possible to procrastinate engaging in sales and sometimes in marketing activities.

Some business owners say things like, 'I don't have to be on the phone talking to people all day. I've got myself and my products and services packaged properly.' Most of us did not start our businesses to sell things. We started them to do something we are passionate about and we have no desire to become one of those dreaded 'sales people.' Many of us struggle between needing sales and looking for an alternative to having sales conversations.

Phoning people is not the only way to produce sales. If you are running a bricks and mortar store, lots of phone calls are not the only way to build your business. Businesses like coaching, speaking and delivering workshops or services may be different. Customers need to move from knowing to trusting before purchasing an intangible service. That often means a conversation, and many times, more than one conversation.

When I take my clothes to my dry cleaner's, that's a tangible purchase. If they're still around after years of service, it means they haven't wrecked too many clothes. I have proof they will take care of my clothes. I hand them dirty clothes and when I come back I can see they are clean. That has clear value and I can see it.

It's harder to see value when you provide an intangible service like teaching skills. If a potential customer has never tried your service and he or she doesn't know anyone who has, there is hesitation to buy. The sales process is different. The sales math is also different and knowing how it's different and how to manage it is critical.

Increase your expertise around sales and marketing in your business. You'll experience more freedom through knowing how your sales math works, and through the growth your business will inevitably experience from you having more conversations with more with potential clients!

Practice Tips:

- Don't fear marketing and sales. Get the training and support you need to become a ninja!
- Spend at least 25% of each business day in sales generating activity. That's about 2 hours per day in an 8-hour day.
- Create games and rewards with any marketing or sales activity you resist, for example, 'If I make 5 sales this week, next week I will go for a mani-pedi.'

- Don't do it alone. Be in regular (daily or hourly) communication with an accountability partner or coach for support.
- Learn something new every day that builds your marketing and sales toolbox.

Habit #8: Become an expert with your marketing and sales math for everything you sell.

FEATURE INTERVIEW

Colin Sprake is a heart-centered Business Sherpa, 4-time Bestselling Author, International Speaker, Trainer and Creator of *The Ultimate Business Success System...with SOUL!*, a 7-Step System to six figures in profits or more in 12 months or less. He is a member of the Transformational Leadership Council (TLC), a committee of 100 of the top transformational leaders in the world led by Jack Canfield.

Colin is a serial entrepreneur and global authority on entrepreneurship having trained over 30,000 entrepreneurs. He's built multiple million dollar businesses globally in various industries and economies. Colin founded *Make Your Mark Training & Consulting* (www.mymsuccess.com) with a passion to assist entrepreneurs in realizing their full revenue and profit potential and doing it with heart, making a positive impression on everyone their business impacts. *Make Your Mark* is currently expanding in Canada, USA and Europe and on track to reaching $250 million in annual revenue by 2020.

What does entrepreneurial freedom mean to you personally?

Entrepreneurial freedom is having the ability to do what I want to do, when I want to do it. I started every business with the intention of having freedom, especially to have the freedom to be able to spend more time with my family. It's the number 1 reason why I do everything that I do.

I don't ever start a business without thinking about the freedom at the end. Freedom is the most important thing – otherwise you become a workaholic and eventually lose everything. Many entrepreneurs are focused on putting a business plan together. They don't put together a *freedom plan* – that is the most important thing.

I'm running a close to 20-million-dollar business and one of the big things for me is I plan all my freedom time every year. If I don't plan it, I spend all my time running around chasing my tail doing business. I forget about the most important thing: My family and why I'm really doing this. A freedom plan is putting your business and your family in one plan.

I put a certain amount of freedom in my schedule each week. When I get to Vancouver, I have the entire afternoon booked off. I'll check with my wife and kids to see if they're around. Sometimes it's, 'Let's go out and have ice cream together, have a chat, sit on the park bench,' or whatever. I love doing that kind of stuff, because I learn so much about my kids and my wife.

Our business tag line is *Business With Soul*. It's about putting your heart and soul into what you do and being a conscious business owner. There is nothing worse than having a very successful business and no support in terms of your family. I want to spend time with my family and not be so addicted to work. I'm addicted to fun and love with my family. I love my business. I love serving people. I serve people and do a great job at it. The bottom line is: I serve them because it gives me the opportunity to have so much flexibility and freedom with my beautiful family.

What three habits contribute the most to you achieving that freedom?

I wake up every single day, open my eyes, look at my wife, and give gratitude for her and everything else in my life. That's the number 1 thing I do. So many of us wake up wanting. We keep wanting stuff – more business, a bigger home, a nicer car. Sadly, that gives us a feeling of lacking. If you keep on feeling lacking, lacking shows up. Give gratitude for everything that you have and the universe gives you more to be grateful for. I live by that. It's my number 1 thing in terms of being successful.

The second thing is about making sure I'm on the right track. I am a big fan of focusing on family, so I spend a lot of time focusing on what needs to be done around my family. I ask myself, *Am I in line with my freedom plan?* I'm also a big fan of dream boarding. I look at my dream board to see if I'm doing something today towards my big dreams. The dreams on my dream boards are not all material. Some of them are family and quality time.

The third thing is, I look in terms of getting to the next level of being an entrepreneur. If you always need to have everything perfect before you do something, you'll probably go broke as an entrepreneur. It's all about jumping off the cliff and building your wings on the way down. Many people don't get this and you have just got to do it. Sometimes you have to take that big bold step. If you don't have discomfort in your life, you'll never get the growth you want. When you have extreme discomfort you'll get extreme growth. Those two are synergistic with one another. I live knowing the more discomfort I have in the day, the more I'm growing.

Give us a picture window into how you start your days.

My day is very structured. I believe there are success principles that people do every day that really get them going. The first thing I do is my gratitude.

I'm not a fan of jumping on my phone or the internet to see what emails came in. I go for a run at least 4 times a week, because fitness is such an important part to me. It's doubled the results of the business in the last 18 months. I love to go out and get some air into my brain. When running I listen to something motivational or from another trainer or expert. You should always be growing and learning. I don't believe you should listen to the news or anything negative. I never turn the TV on in the morning or watch the news. I think it's the craziest thing people do. They watch negative stuff and then the whole day starts off that way. I love listening to stuff that really motivates, inspires and takes me to the next level. Sometimes I come sprinting home because I have one amazing nugget that I can't wait to write down and use in my business or my life. One of my favourite things is learning how to improve communication. Because you can either be 'right' or you can be in a relationship.

What's the most important habit entrepreneurs should have?

The number one thing for me is getting stuff done. Don't overthink things, don't sit and procrastinate, don't get analysis paralysis. You have to analyze things and look at the risks. But, you have got to take action and that's where most people do not get ahead. They're so busy, so scared and so fearful. The biggest thing to do is jump through the fear. Fear is just stuff you made up in your head about a situation. Move forward and you'll always be successful. I always say, *What I get done in a day, the average person gets done in a week*. Why? Because I'm not thinking about stuff. I want a t-shirt made that says *'Don't Think'* because thinking causes a lot of our problems.

Any final thoughts to share about entrepreneurial freedom?

Remember why you are doing it, and ask yourself, *How much is enough?* The big thing for me is this: You can keep on making more and more money, as long as you are not also working more and more hours. Have people come in and trust them. That's a big thing for entrepreneurs; to trust people to do things for you and work with them. Show them how to do things so that you can grow financially and also grow your time off. That's why we truly do it. I'm not here to work harder in the next 5 to 10 years. I want to work smarter, have more people on board and put my trust in them. Will they ever do it exactly the way I want? Probably not. They'll probably do it better because they're more of a specialist. That gives me time off with my family because that's really why I do it. There are two key questions that every one of the entrepreneurs reading your book should be asking themselves. *How much money is enough? And how much time do I want off?* Then the 3rd question is, *Why am I doing this?*

CHAPTER **TWO**

ORGANIZE

168

'There is a difference between knowing the path and walking the path.'
Morpheus, captain of the Nebuchadnezzar (*The Matrix*)

What you and I know is that there are 24 hours in a day and 7 days in a week. That means there are 168 hours in every single week of the year. Entrepreneurs know this fact with certainty. And knowing makes absolutely no difference in achieving freedom.

You have the same amount of time in your week as I have in mine. So does Tim Ferris who wrote *The 4-Hour Work Week*. Barak Obama leads an entire country with 168 hours in his week. Last week, Richard Branson ran his multi-billion dollar empire with the same amount of time as you. Despite this fact, why do some people get so much less accomplished in their 168 hours than others?

It almost seems like there are two groups of people: People who are successful and accomplish much and those who do not. Both have 168 hours, so there must be something that the successful people know and do that the others don't.

As I look at the habits of successful entrepreneurs there are certain things that they have in common. One habit they have is they vigorously protect non-negotiable items in their calendar. You have to eat – that is non-negotiable. I don't care if you are Barak Obama or Damian Reid, you need

45

food. You also have to sleep – that's also non-negotiable. The exact amount you need we will address later in Habit #49.

I include daily meditation, endurance training and spiritual practice in my non-negotiables. I'm training for my first Ironman two years from now. Sleeping and eating are two things I now mess with even less because of that. There is time in my calendar scheduled for all of these non-negotiable activities.

The first thing you need to do with your 168 hours is take the non-negotiable time out of what you consider available time your calendar. When you are committed, you spend the time on your non-negotiables whether you schedule them or not.

Sometimes this gets a little scary for entrepreneurs to see in reality. If I sleep 7 hours x 7 days that's 49 hours. Take sleep out of my 168 – that leaves my week with 119 hours. Take out an hour a day to eat and now I am down to 112 hours a week. And we just got started! Then take personal care like showering, shaving, etc., out at 30 minutes a day, and we are down to 108.5 hours.

Now, in my case, take time out for my spiritual practice and meditation. At 45 minutes a day, that's another 5.25 hours. And we haven't touched my workouts at 8 hours a week. Quickly the hours go down and you have whatever is left to play with. In my case, I now have just over 95 hours remaining.

I was having this conversation with a client and she said, 'How do people manage to work 80 hour weeks?!' My answer: Simple. They start to trash the non-negotiables. They sleep 4 hours a night, skip meals, eat fast food and don't spend time with their family or loved ones. Then they wonder why their life doesn't work and why they don't have the freedom they want as an entrepreneur.

There are two things to watch out for here: One is to not turn your back on the things that are most important to you. Keep your non-negotiables *non-negotiable*. The second thing to watch out for is what you're doing with the remaining time left over. What do you do with the time that's left once you account for the things that are most important? You can get into trouble if you put the wrong things into your calendar next.

There's a story that has been around for a while that illustrates how to schedule your time in the best way possible. It's about a teacher who walks into a classroom with a large glass container. He fills it with big, fist-sized rocks and asks the class if the container is full. When they say yes, he pours gravel between the rocks and asks the question again. He repeats this twice more with sand and water. The story demonstrates that if you start with the water, sand or gravel you will never fit the big rocks.

Consider the jar is the 168 hours in your life every week. Entrepreneurs typically start to fill their jar with small things like the gravel first. You deal first with the fire that is burning today, time suckers, things you hate, things you are not good at and the like. You don't do the things that will make the *biggest difference* FIRST. At the end of the week you find yourself wondering why you're scrambling to fulfill all of your commitments.

There isn't a one-size-fits-all way to do this. I have seen various successful approaches. Some people spend two uninterrupted hours at the beginning of every day on the one thing that will make the biggest impact. I've also seen people who 'swallow the frog first.' They do the ickiest task that they hate or resist at the beginning of the day. Once they overcome that challenge, the rest of the day is smooth sailing. For many entrepreneurs, this looks like some version of doing the kind of sales work we talked about in Habit #8.

A good practice is to schedule large, general blocks of time in your calendar. Look 2-3 weeks out from today and put important big items in even though you may not know the details right now. These blocks could be things like 'Sales,' 'Networking,' 'Blog Writing,' 'Planning,' 'Biggest Difference Maker,' etc.

When you get close to the 'Biggest Difference Maker,' time block, you decide then what is the most important. Are you going to launch your new program? Find sponsors? Spend the time on sales? Do what is going to make the biggest difference to your business at that point, or, absolutely equally important, what is going to make the biggest difference to your level of energy and state of mind.

Set up your 168 hours based on your priorities in your business and in other areas of your life. You'll experience a tremendous amount of freedom simply from knowing exactly how you're spending these hours and from making the most of them.

Practice Tips:

- Schedule all your non-negotiables in your calendar first.

- Get your big rocks into your calendar after your non-negotiables.
- Start your day working on the one thing that will make the biggest difference – 'eat the frog.'
- Schedule big chunks in your calendar 2-3 weeks ahead to leave room for the big rocks.
- What new non-negotiables would make the biggest difference for you, like meditation for example? Put them in your calendar.

Habit #9: Schedule your non-negotiables in your calendar then manage your life with the time remaining.

Your Life Is A Match For Your Environment

'If a cluttered desk is a sign of a cluttered mind, of what, then, is an empty desk a sign?'
~ Albert Einstein, theoretical physicist

The environment you are in has an immediate impact on how you think, feel, act, work and live. Having your physical environment—both your home and workspaces (in some cases they are the same)—organized and functional is critical to experiencing freedom.

I have a friend in New York who has invested lots of time and money in organizing her physical environment. Three years ago she made a decision to live with her parents again. She recognized that they were advancing in age and needed more support with their day-to-day life. And, the New York rental market was just booming and she could make more money renting her apartment.

She packed up her two-bedroom apartment and fit everything into two rooms of her parents' townhouse. She dumped all her stuff in the basement, went to IKEA and got her new space setup. Despite the new furniture and organization, the space still did not feel like her own. The environment was not conducive to creating peace and freedom. She felt like she had just come back from college and dumped stuff here and there. It felt like a transient space.

About 4 months ago, she really took a look at the space because she felt like it had no flow. It felt like there was always something to climb over even though she didn't have a lot of things. She noticed that's how her experience of her business started to feel. It was like she was always having to climb over something or get over something.

One weekend my friend decided to do something different. She shut her phone off and told her parents, 'Don't bother me. I'm here but I'm not.' She started with taking all the stuff off the shelves, piled it in the middle of the room and started moving the furniture. She completely reorganized her living, working and sleeping spaces.

Before reorganizing, everything was being blocked and she couldn't see into one particular area. It felt like she was hiding places in her space. Everything now has an open and airy flow. You can see from one side of the room to the next. There are dividers in the rooms but nothing is blocking anything.

Not surprisingly, her life was a reflection of the condition of her environment. One area would be working but she would discover she was hiding another area. Her entire experience of living her life in the same space but a new environment has now altered. Now she wakes up in the morning to the sunlight. Before she needed her alarm.

And it is by no means all done. She is very clear that it is an ongoing process to attend to her environment. She is still sorting through papers. However, now it's much more enjoyable than before. Now she finds that can sit down, watch TV and shred paper at the same time. She's noticed interesting new things like being able to watch more television now than she has watched in the last five years. She is now able to work while she is watching and she really enjoys it. Now she loves working in her space because it is an altered environment.

Not long ago I experienced something similar. My primary office workspace is a minimalist desk with a kneeling chair. It only takes a few file folders and one to-do pile to make it almost impossible to find space for my laptop and notebook.

I began avoiding working at my desk and started to relocate to other places in my home. My favourite spot on the couch was bad for my posture and gave me backaches. Finally, I bit the bullet (in truth it took me 10 minutes) and cleared up my workspace. The effect was immediate and I felt grounded. I saw corresponding results in my productivity and focus.

Having your physical space organized is as much a mental and emotional thing as it is physical. When your environment is cluttered that gets reflected – it's what shows up in your life. It's amazing how many entrepreneurs work somewhere other than their desk because their desk is cluttered.

Environment is one of the Key Areas of Life that we will delve into with more details in Chapter 4. The challenge I see with many entrepreneurs is that this area does not get focus or attention because the importance and impact is not clear. If someone said every stray paper on your desk costs you $1,000 a month in income, it would probably get organized.

What *is* the cost of having a lack of organization in your environment? What does it cost you in terms of freedom? As my New York friend discovered, her life and her business seemed to be correlated to the condition of her environment. When my desk is cluttered, I experience very little freedom or creativity in my business.

Yes absolutely, making the time for one more habit called Organizing Your Environment may seem like a colossal waste of time. It may seem trivial and unimportant. You may be one of those people who say that you work much better in a messy environment. I have never met someone for whom that was really true. Without exception, every person I have ever worked with who organized their environment found that they worked more efficiently and effectively afterward.

Take the time to create an environment that promotes clarity. Have your environment support you in flowing seamlessly into what there is to work on next. Have everything you need to do your work right there in front of you. When I am working on something, what I need next is already there waiting for me. Everything has a place, I know where it is and I work on it when it's time to work on it. When I am not working on it, it has a place where it lives until it's time to work on it again.

If you are not someone who likes to organize and create order, hire someone who does. We're going to delve a little deeper into that two habits from now. There are organized people all around you that would love to get their hands on your chaotic environment. They are the ones who can't help themselves and have probably already commented on what they could do to help you create order at the first sight of your desk or office.

Once your space is organized, make sure your desk doesn't become the storage space for something else. Have the spaces in your environment—both business and personal—have intention and purpose. Keep the space you are going to work in as a sacred space for your personal expression.

It's amazing to me the number of entrepreneurs I come across who are ashamed when people come to their desk or see where they work. Or, on the opposite side of the same coin, they say things like, 'My desk is always a mess,' like it's a badge of honour or the way it is supposed to be. If you find yourself saying this, consider: Why do you think other things aren't working in your business?

Take on cleaning up your work and personal spaces, or hire someone to organize them for you. You'll be pleasantly surprised at the results!

Practice Tips:

- Personalize your workspace to fit *you* rather then you trying to fit yourself *into your space*. It's your domain – it should be a reflection of you.
- Your workspace does not have to look like offices in the corporations you used to work for. You really get to say how it goes.
- Keep your desk ready for guests. Try imagining that your most sought after client could walk through the door at any minute and that you could invite them to spend a few hours working with you in your space.
- Have everything you need in order to do the work for the day in your work area.
- Everything has a place. When you're not using something, put it back in its home.

Habit #10: Create and design your work environment to match the results you are committed to producing.

Stop Doing The Tasks You Hate

'The only way to be truly satisfied is to do what you believe is great work. And the only way to do great work is to love what you do.'
~ Steve Jobs, co-founder, chairman and CEO of *Apple Inc.*

Let's reverse the second sentence of the Steve Jobs quote above to say: 'The only way to do crappy work is to do what you hate.' This is equally as true as the original quote. When people work on things they hate, the quality of their work diminishes and they experience less freedom.

My brand portrait photographer, Cynthia Phillip, shot the cover and about the author photos for this book. When she first had the idea of becoming a photographer, she would say, 'I want to be a photographer but I don't know what to shoot. So I'm just going to shoot everything and call myself a photographer.'

Cynthia found herself frustrated because nothing she was doing would satisfy her. She took pictures of babies and pregnant moms, took pictures at engagements, showers, parties and baptisms and basically shot just about anything. She thought, *I have to take photos of everything. Because that's what photographers do.*

She was putting out nice photos but everything else that comes with a great photo wasn't there. She wasn't excited about her work because she felt 'blah' about it. Cynthia kept finding herself in a box with everyone else. Her work looked like anybody's work. Did her clients like the pictures? Yes, they were happy. And at the same time, no one was jumping up and down saying, 'This is the most amazing photo of myself I have ever seen!'

Cynthia's story is not unique among the entrepreneurial community. Many entrepreneurs start businesses to pursue their passion or do more of what they love. Then they fall into the trap of thinking that they have to do *everything* in their business.

It's important to identify the tasks that you dislike or hate doing. They are the parts of your day that you dread, or worse, put off doing all together. Time spent on activities you are not fond of gives you *experiences*. It does not, however, give you *freedom*. Entrepreneurs often feel trapped, anxious, overwhelmed and even resentful about the approaching times they've allotted to certain tasks in their business.

I find the most resistance from my clients when we start talking about *cost*. Cost involves more than just financial cost, as we will see in Habit #12. What does it cost you to keep doing these tasks you dislike? What effect does it have on the quality of the work you produce?

The first thing to do is create a list of the tasks you hate doing. The great news is that for everything you dislike, someone out there loves and even thrives on doing it. For example, I hate filing. To me, it's a tedious task. Left on my own, I will grow a pile of unfiled paper 4 inches high. One of my project managers gets sheer joy out of filing. She loves making labels and all things related to organization.

If you don't know someone who loves to do the tasks on your list, there are many places to find people. Some of my favourites include sites like *Kijiji*, *Fiverr* and *Upwork*. Young members of your family or the children of friends may have design or social media skills. And, they would probably love to earn some extra money.

It's important to learn to trust yourself in deciding whether or not a task is yours to do. Sometimes entrepreneurs feel they have to do things because it's a rite of passage. We think we have to suffer through aspects of our business if we ever hope to reap the rewards of success and freedom. No one said being an entrepreneur is easy. But you don't have to suffer through things you really dislike. Your business doesn't have to be painful. It's not a sign of weakness to outsource tasks that make more sense to be done by others. It's a sign of working smart. There are many alternatives to struggling through the tasks you dislike.

And just because you know how to do something doesn't mean you are going to necessarily like it, or that you should do it yourself. For example, I'm great at math, reports, analysis, spreadsheets and budgets. I have all the skills required to do the accounting work for my business. If I put my mind to it, I could do it. And yet I find bookkeeping tedious and boring work. It takes me a long time to complete these tasks in this area because I am constantly stopping to do something else. That would still be the case today if I didn't hire a bookkeeper.

So what happened to Cynthia's photography business? One day out of the blue a friend Paula said, 'I am going to New York. I am going to buy some crazy, wacky clothes and would love to stand in front of your camera and see what we create.' Cynthia trusted the process and went along for the ride. Later in the trip, Paula suggested doing some intimate shots. Cynthia said, 'I don't know. I usually only take photos of babies, bellies and engagements and what not. So I really don't know if I could actually provide you with what you are looking for…but let's have fun anyways.'

At the end of the 8-hour photoshoot, Cynthia discovered what it meant to specialize. She realized she had been wasting her time shooting everything just because she thought she had to. She had been avoiding becoming a niche photographer because she thought she would fail. She was shooting things just because they looked good even though she didn't feel good about it.

The photoshoot with Paula was a discovery of what Cynthia loved completely by accident. Paula stood in front of the camera and did things and Cynthia found herself guiding herself and telling herself what to do. Cynthia's sister was at the photoshoot and said to her, 'I have never seen this side of you. Something just completely opened up.'

At that moment the doors of creativity flew wide open and for the past five years Cynthia pursued her passion. She has been photographing women in her unique shooting style ever since. And her business expanded massively. She started to do really, really well because she loved it! Every shot was unique and special. It all came from her passion for her work. Who she was and how she was taking the photos made the images—regardless of the shoot locations or the people in front of the camera—look amazing.

She discovered it had nothing to do with her camera and equipment. She started taking shots with her *iPhone* and even with a polaroid camera. She noticed that the image quality was of course different, but that the artistic expression and imagery stayed the same. She knew it was the change in *her* that made the difference and not the tools. That was an eye-opening discovery for her because she used to think she needed the perfect tools: The best camera, the best lens, the best lighting, the best of this, the best of that… And she discovered that the success of her business depended instead on her giving herself the freedom to do only what she loved.

Today, Cynthia's days of shooting boudoir photography are over. The chapter reached the end of its natural life cycle and she came to not enjoy doing it any more. She made the choice to stop that line of business because her passion evolved. She decided to pivot again to something she loves.

She found next that she has a passion for telling a story through business photographs; that she wanted to disrupt the world of traditional business headshots. She took aspects of storytelling that she loved in boudoir and brought it into business. I am not only a current client of hers, I know several of her clients personally. Her process and her work is pure genius. The personal branded portrait work that she does now is even more fulfilling to her and again, she loves it.

She continues to look at her business for things she doesn't enjoy doing and for ways to get them managed. She recognizes the need for a system to manage her interactions with clients so that this aspect of her business flows more easily. There's a part of the administration process in her business that she doesn't like doing, and she also recognizes now that her time and energy are better spent doing what she loves and is best at – taking amazing, passion-inspired pictures. So she's looking into hiring an assistant to manage that part for her, so she can focus on the good stuff.

Start delegating the tasks you don't like doing in your business, so you can do the same.

Practice Tips:

- Make a list of all of the tasks you hate and the ones that feel like they deplete your energy.
- Locate people in your network who love doing those tasks. Use job sites like *Fiverr.com* or *Upwork.com*, or post ads in *Kijiji* or *Craigslist*.
- Hire an assistant and ask them to support you in doing the tasks you dislike.
- Listen to your feelings about something and your gut. Trust yourself.
- Keep looking on a monthly basis to see if there are any new tasks you need to add to your list to outsource.

Habit #11: Identify the tasks you hate and give them to someone who loves doing them.

Honour Your Zone of Genius

'Talent hits a target no one else can hit; Genius hits a target no one else can see.'
~ Arthur Schopenhauer, philosopher

This habit is closely connected to the last one. Often, the things we dislike doing are also things we're not great at.

We know that the rate of failure in the first years for small businesses is quite high. In my experience, one of the reasons for this is because people fail to delegate. Delegation is critical. An entrepreneur often wears almost all the hats of running a business, especially in the first couple of years. And the reality is that not everybody is good at everything.

Take bookkeeping as an example. I am a terrible bookkeeper and do not have the experience to do the type of bookkeeping *Amorvita* needs.

For the first couple years of my business, I tried to do my own bookkeeping and accounting. It was the worst part of working my business. My reporting to the tax offices was always behind. Monthly reporting inside our accounting software was always incomplete. I was operating my business with an incomplete picture of its performance. This is dangerous and a fast path to business failure. The not-so-funny thing about this is that I was not following my own coaching in this area. And predictably, I was dealing with the same issues that my clients were.

Sometimes we don't dislike the tasks we aren't good at. This can be an even harder pitfall to avoid. You may not hate these tasks – it's possible that you even *like* these tasks. And yet you're not great at doing them. Although you may be reluctant to at first, you'll find freedom in letting them go. They are tasks that have you working outside your *Zone of Genius*.

Think of those times when you're in the zone, performing in your business and you wish you could stay in that zone forever. You're on a roll. You have a feeling of euphoria combined with challenge, ease, and excitement. Feeling that way is a sign that whatever you're working on is the kind of work that you're supposed to be doing. Design the time you spend working in and on your business to allow you to be in that zone as much as possible. It comes down to doing tasks that leverage your talents in combination with your purpose.

Say I hire a bookkeeper for $40 an hour to do the 5 hours of booking I try to do every month. Not only will it get done faster, but now I have time to focus on other tasks in my Zone of Genius. Let's say that bookkeeper doubles my efficiency and gets the work done in 2.5 hours. It costs me $100 and I gain 5 hours of time every month. If my billable hourly rate for my services was $150 an hour, I just created an opportunity to earn an extra $750 per month and it only cost me $100. I just increased my bottom line by net $650 per month. I certainly have an experience of increased freedom in my business.

There are a couple of things that are like bookkeeping for me. Another of my weaknesses is working inside *Infusionsoft*. I am a complete closet geek and love playing with *Infusionsoft* campaigns and design. But I'm not great at it and I think it's fair to say I'm not even *good* at it. When I first got the software, I spent 3 hours working on a particular campaign. It was not a complicated campaign but I pressed the wrong button and deleted all the work I had done. That was the day I decided to hire my *Infusionsoft* administrator.

She is not 'cheap' but is worth every penny I spend. Not only does she make suggestions and create things in ways that I don't even know exist, she accomplishes what I was accomplishing in about 20% of the time I was spending. I am left with more time to coach, create and design ways for entrepreneurs to have more freedom in their lives – my zone of genius. Don't leave me to run *Infusionsoft* – that's just a bad idea. And don't even get me started on the times when I think I should work on our creative and graphic design work. That's even worse than *Infusionsoft*!

It's important to take an honest look at what you are and aren't great at. One of the first investments I made when I started *Amorvita* was hiring a brilliant designer named Jeff Kahane. He had done work for the Vancouver Olympics. Jeff is the genius behind the creation of the *Amorvita* logo and brand identity. The work he did was amazing and I was so pleased. I can only imagine what it would have looked like if I had played amateur graphic designer. I always get compliments on the logo and the feel of the brand. The logo has so much depth to it and it captures so much meaning. Every time I look at the logo, I know how much thought went into the elements and it never gets boring.

It's very important to take care to outsource your work to the right person or people. There's a time and place for going to *Fiverr.com* or a similar site for logo design. It's not always necessary to spend hundreds or thousands of dollars to get a great logo design that's perfect for your brand. A great example of this kind of logo is if you are doing a webinar and want a logo specifically for that event. You can provide the source your brand guidelines and style sheet and ask for a design that's consistent with them. However, when you're establishing the optics and visual identity of your company that's not a time to go to *Fiverr* – you'd definitely want to make a higher investment.

When delegating you need to be selective and use your common sense. I still see a lot of seasoned business owners who know they should be delegating still hanging on to things. This is not a 'one and done' habit. It's an ongoing habit to keep looking to see, 'What am I not good at? Who is better at this than I am that I can hire so I can focus instead on what I *am* good at?'

And equally importantly, once you've let it go, keep your hands off it. One of the biggest ways business owners get in their own way is to delegate, and then take the task back a little bit at a time. At some point you need to trust your resources. Trust yourself that you chose good quality resources. Be wary of your unconscious efforts to relinquish control. It chips away from time in your Zone of Genius and disempowers your support resources.

This continues to be an ongoing area of development for me. One of the challenges I have in this area is remembering that although delegation takes time, it saves time in the long run. It's a matter of short-term versus long-term gain. When I get into a time crunch, I tend to think to myself, *I'll just do it in 5 minutes. I could take this 5 minutes to explain what I need done to someone, and it might take 20 minutes for that person to do it. But if I just do it now myself this one time, I can get what I need* right now… It starts me down a slippery slope.

I've learned it takes *trust*. Trust the team you hired. Trust the process. Allow yourself the space to empower and delegate things to people and then give them the space to pick those things up and run with them. There is a tremendous amount of freedom available in doing so.

Practice Tips:

- Ask people already on your team to support you in identifying what you're not great at. Don't take their opinions personally.
- Catch yourself when you say something like, *It's faster for me to do this myself.* Delegate that thing.
- Keep a list of all the things that are outside your Zone of Genius. These are things you will know to delegate.
- Spend as much of your day as possible working in your Zone of Genius.
- Keep track of how much money you add to your bottom line by delegating what you're not great at.

Habit #12: List of all the tasks you do that you are not great at and plan to delegate them all with specific deadlines.

Free Yourself Of Time Suckers

'Dost thou love life? Then do not squander time, for that is the stuff life is made of.'
~ Benjamin Franklin, one of the Founding Fathers of the United States

In Habit #11, we talked about things that you hate to do and why you should let them go. In contrast, however, time suckers are things that you like or maybe even love to do but you have NO BUSINESS doing them. They often show up when you're procrastinating. They're those irrelevant tasks and time wasters.

One popular time sucker for entrepreneurs seems to be social media. Now

I'm not saying that all social media is time sucking behaviour. There are some legitimate things to be spending time doing on social media. But you know what I'm talking about here – it's those few minutes you're going to spend on *Facebook* before you start your sales calls. Or that extra time you added to your break to browse your *Twitter* or *Instagram* feeds.

There are some common time suckers that I find among clients. People seem to love to send emails back and forth 3 or 4 times to schedule appointments. Why waste time doing this?! Get yourself connected to your clients with scheduling software like *Timetrade*. It integrates directly with your calendar and offers people your available times. There are a many other scheduling solutions out there. I love the ability to offer different types of appointments through my scheduling software. I have separate links for in-person meetings, coaching calls and introductory calls.

Another common time sucker: Spending time on travel sites booking your own travel. You could have someone do that for you – for free! It can take hours to research and book travel.

Texting and other forms of messaging – more time suckers. Do you love starting interesting text conversations in the middle of tasks you're working on?

I'm often asked, 'How do I find the time suckers in my life? Where are places to looks for them?' First, look at your default actions when you are avoiding work. What are the things you do instead of working on what there is to work on? What are your bad habits you feel you have little control over? Another place to look: What are some of the things that other people keep telling you you could do faster? These are all great places to find time suckers.

If you don't trust yourself to manage your time suckers, add productivity apps to your life. The app world is constantly evolving. We keep our favourites on the *Resource* page of the *Amorvita* website (amorvita.ca/resources).

Here are some of the major types of apps you may find useful:

- **Website Blockers**: Create distraction-free periods in your workday by blocking certain websites. Block access to emails, social media, or other sites. Some allow you to schedule blocks of times in advance.
- **Ad and Newsfeed Eliminators**: Replace newsfeed or online ads

with inspirational quotes and pictures.

- **Bookmarking**: Stop being distracted by the latest thing that crosses your screen. These apps allow you to save interesting articles, websites, etc., to one place so that you can review them at a later time.
- **Timers**: These have many different uses. Manage time using the *Pomodoro Technique*, developed by Francesco Cirillo in the late 1980s, which divides time into intervals. Track time on individual tasks and more.

Timers help get rid of time suckers. It's important to understand how long it actually takes to complete tasks. I've discovered that entrepreneurs have no idea how long it actually takes them to do things. Or, they live in a fantasy world when it comes to scheduling things. And I am not immune to this. In fact I just did it this morning.

I scheduled 90 minutes to work on the company newsletter. I knew that I needed to finish my blog post before I could start the newsletter. I thought to myself, *I will complete the entire newsletter plus finish the blog post in 90 minutes.* Usually it takes about 2 hours to do a newsletter and 30 minutes to do a tune-up on a blog post. So there I go scheduling 90 minutes to do a 150-minute task. Of course, 90 minutes later…*Ding ding ding!!!* the alarm goes off and I'm not finished.

Timers allow you to get clear about how long things take. That's step number one. Step two is then scheduling the appropriate amount of time to get that work done. The final step is to add in extra time to plan for the unexpected. You are going to have situations where unexpected things come up. You need to schedule time *in between* the times in your calendar to allow for that. Sometimes the phone will ring and it's a call that you need to take now instead of calling back later. Without extra space to leave room for things like that to happen, 10 minutes on that call ends up being 10 minutes not working on whatever you had scheduled during that time.

If you take this on, you'll notice that your experience of freedom in your workday will increase. You'll also notice more freedom and more available time on the days you schedule off. You'll have more time to relax on those days because you will have completed everything you had to complete during your workdays. You may begin to experience time differently and feel like you have more time. We already talked about the fact that there are exactly 168 hours in a week. When you're scheduling your work in a realistic way and leaving time for the unexpected to arise, you get to do focused work on a regular basis. By just implementing this new way of scheduling, chances are you will rid yourself of most of your time suckers. You'll get things done in the times you allocate for them and you won't have to carry stuff over into your evenings and weekends.

I want to say one last thing here: Time suckers are not always 'bad' things. I always want to do less work when my 19-year-old daughter is around. I'm not sure if that ever changes as a parent. We love to spend time with our kids, but sometimes they distract us from staying on schedule and staying focused. Even though this qualifies as a time sucker, it's not a bad thing that we want to spend time with the people we love. A way to have the best of both worlds is to make sure we schedule time to spend with our loved ones when we know they are going to visit. This way, we can give them our undivided attention and be fully present when we're with them, and we can also make sure everything in our business gets done during the other times.

Practice Tips:

- Use timers to clearly understand how long tasks *actually* take to complete. Once you know, schedule that amount of time in your calendar and not less.
- Plan for the unexpected by leaving some space in your calendar between appointments and tasks.
- Give tasks that you find are time suckers for you, but that still need to be done, away to someone else to complete.
- Use automation and apps to support you in remaining focused.
- Be forgiving with yourself when you find yourself spending time on a time sucker. Put structures in place to not repeat doing so.

Habit #13: Identify your favourite time suckers and either get rid of them or schedule (and stick to!) appropriate times for them.

Implement Workflow Processes

'If you can't describe what you are doing as a process, you don't know what you're doing.'
~ W. Edwards Deming, engineer, statistician, professor, author, lecturer and management consultant

This habit is all about repetitive tasks, automation, checklists and streamlining things, both in your professional and personal life. Without checklists, automation and flow, the feeling of overwhelm is just around the corner (that's assuming it hasn't already arrived). Without processes, the experience of your freedom draining away is almost inevitable.

I was having a chat with one of my colleagues Kim McLaughlin about this. Kim runs *Lyra Communications*, a social media company, out of Toronto. She shared that while social media is fun, creative and engaging, at a basic level it's a collection of many tasks. If her team falls down on those tasks social media doesn't happen. It doesn't matter how creative they are or what the quality of the content is. Their success is in the *execution*.

When she started to expand her business she had to build her team. Workflow was important because social media has so many different tiny moving parts. Kim learned the hard way how to put workflow in place between all of the moving parts. First, she discovered that you cannot take anything for granted. No one can read your mind or anticipate what is going to happen next.

She set about drawing a map of every single path in the operation of her business – every action for a tweet to go live, a *Facebook* post to happen or a *Facebook* ad to go up. For blogs, the process includes conceptualizing, writing an outline, the actual writing, the approval of it, editing, the proofing of it, how the client is involved, etc. Every single task and step is documented including what software is used, deadlines and who approves what.

She discovered by doing this how critical her workflow maps are to her business. They are not static documents and are constantly getting revamped. She learned the hard way that when she leaves out pieces that are 'obvious' to her, they never are to someone else. When working with clients to deliver social media programs, she has two sets of workflows: An internal one to deliver the program, and one for the client to outline a clear set of expectations.

Everything that has to happen in your business needs to be documented step by step. It's important to include who is responsible and what and when things need to happen. The easiest way to do this is to draw a picture or map. I use a free software program called *ClickCharts* to map out my process flow. I recently relaunched the *Amorvita* Associate partner program that has many moving parts. I had to draw the entire program so I could be clear on it and see it all laid out in front of me before implementation.

Start documenting your workflow processes from the time you start your business. Or, if you didn't, start now. Many of your business task sequences are repetitive. Don't make up the process over and over again. It's easier to work from a checklist and save yourself time and mental effort. I manage a lot from checklists. Once you have a complete checklist, it's easy to delegate the process and train using the checklist. When you go to hire for your team, you'll need job descriptions. These will be based on your workflow and what is required to support each of the business processes in your map.

Having your workflow documented supports the scalability of your business. If you're selling a product your workflow may include many steps. For example:

- What you order
- Who you order from
- On which date of the month you place the order
- How you place the order (for example, is it by email?)
- What information you provide
- What the supplier does
- What you need to approve and send back
- When the product arrives
- The unpacking and inspecting procedure
- The procedure for repackaging with North American labels
- The procedure for making a sale
- How does that sale gets communicated to your staff
- What happens next...

As your business grows and you expand, because everything is documented, the planning and execution of the expansion becomes much easier.

Another reason to put in place workflow processes is to manage the 'hit by a bus' factor. Your business needs to be able to run without you. It should be able to fully function on its own. One key factor in making your business saleable is the integrity and stability of the processes created. What's being sold is the *processes*. If the processes live in your head, no one can replicate your business. No one wants to buy a business that lives in another person's head.

This is a crucial aspect of having a mature, saleable business. You want to be able to say, 'Go to these binders and these files and here are the passwords.' From documented, scalable business practices you can start to build management plans and contingency plans.

Ideally your workflow will have already been outlined in your business plan, but in practice that may not be the case. The first year when you're in the trenches, things change. You think you know what you're doing when you write the business plan before you launch. It's not until you get on the court that you know what your clients *actually* need. You learn along the way that the processes you laid out need tweaking and that at times you need to switch and do something another way.

I didn't figure out the need to document processes until it was too late. I started to feel the pain when things started to fall through the cracks. I made the mistake of assuming that my team knew what I was thinking. I would communicate 80% of something and leave out 20%. I would either forget to outline or explain something or I would assume they would already know how to do it. Tasks don't magically get done just because you have a team. The people on your team may have the best of intentions – fundamentally I believe people want to do a good job. But the processes need to be clear. Having a documented workflow is a great way to empower your team to do what your company needs. This way you can all be successful and you can all share in the rewards of the success. And each person on your team feels good that they have delivered what you need.

Begin to think of everything in your business in terms of workflow processes. When you can automate and scale your business, you get freed up immensely.

Practice Tips:

- Start documenting your workflow processes from the start of your business, or begin now.
- Start today and document any workflow processes not already documented in your business.
- Create job descriptions from your workflow processes.
- Hire your team based on their strengths and ability to deliver and fulfill on your processes.
- Operate from the perspective: *If I got hit by a bus or sold my business tomorrow, what does someone need in order to be able to run it without me?*

Habit #14: Document, map and operate your business using workflow processes.

A Chain Is Only As Strong As Its Weakest Link

'The secret to successful hiring is this: Look for the people who want to change the world.'
~ Marc Benioff, internet entrepreneur, author and philanthropist, founder, chairman and CEO of *Salesforce*

At some point, preferably early on in your business, you are going to create a team and then add members to your team. They will support you with the tasks you hate and the things you aren't good at, free you of your time suckers and more. A workable team enables entrepreneurs to have freedom.

A strong team is a group of individuals who work well together. Nurturing a team nurtures your business. Learning how to create and manage an effective team is critical to the growth of your business. There is a limit to how far you can get on your own.

One of my close friends spent many years working for a famous international company. The company is known for delivering excellent, consistent service through its close to 200,000 employees. We spent time one day chatting about what works and what doesn't work in terms of how teams function.

One thing that doesn't work is if entrepreneurs or business owners have no human connection to their team. It doesn't work to relate to your team members as organizational roles and not as individual human beings. You need to understand what motivates individuals on the team and what makes them tick. When you operate from this place, it can help you manage in a way that facilitates teamwork. Everyone feels loved and appreciated which has them want to be part of the team and do their best work.

One of the best examples I have ever seen of this is in Colin Sprake's company, *Make Your Mark*, based in Vancouver. At a recent conference, he shared some of the practices they incorporate into their team. The list includes having a wall in their office that everybody can see. It has the team's dreams, their Feng Shui profiles, their DISC profiles and what they each want to accomplish. They also have a comprehensive process for bringing new team members on board. Their day-to-day team workflows and processes are impressive, and create team cohesion and individual fulfillment and work satisfaction.

Colin is definitely focused on the human being and not the role. He is focused on every team member fulfilling their dreams. Sometimes there comes a point where the dreams of that team member and the needs of the company diverge. Then they both know it's time for them to part ways. But is there a better way to have a member of your team leave than to know that you made a difference in them achieving what matters to them? I don't think so.

It's important to know what motivates each member of your team. For some people, it's having as much time as possible to spend with their family. Others need to have a bonus to work toward. Some need vacation time. And some people on your team will not care about any of those things. They just want to know themselves that they're doing a good job.

In addition to not having a human connection with your team, here are some other things that don't work:

- Being a dictator
- Putting in structures without checking in with your team
- Not ever checking in with your team
- Not being value focused
- Not creating 'water cooler time' especially if it's a virtual team

When I first heard of the concept of creating water cooler time, I found it interesting. It was something I hadn't considered before. Many micro businesses, home-based entrepreneurs and solopreneurs work with virtual teams. When working with virtual teams, often the meetings focus on the action items required. Conversations about personal matters are limited.

There is nothing wrong with having an effective meeting and remaining productive. Yet, it misses an important opportunity. In an office, water cooler time happens when the team has lunch together, or when people gather and chat in common areas.

Water cooler time gives people freedom to chit-chat about their lives – especially when the boss is not there. They find out what makes each other tick which motivates them to want to support each other. This creates a teamwork atmosphere that is personally motivated – it forms organically and is not something a manager can create.

However, when everything is virtual, a manager needs to create the structure for it to happen. Without that, it's likely that it won't. With a virtual team, purposefully create the time. If you have a 30-minute meeting every Monday morning, let the team know that you will join after 10 minutes. Those first 10 minutes is for them to talk about their weekend and decompress. Sometimes they'll update each other on things they don't want you to hear about or on personal things.

This got me thinking about our team. *Amorvita's* entire Associate structure is virtual. Our Associates work from their individual locations around the world. Twice a month we have co-working days. The Toronto Associates meet in person and we include the others by means of video conference. There are also structures built in for the Associates to be in communication with each other in between meetings. I can now see the opportunity to enhance connection across my team even further.

Our staff team is also quite virtual. Our social media manager, our interns and our project and event managers also work from around the world. I'm always paying attention to how I can create opportunities to support us remaining a strong, cohesive team. I see a similar need in other small businesses. Many entrepreneurs are creating teams that work from different locations. It's important for us to provide the leadership to foster water cooler time, even if virtual.

The first place to start is to lead by example in your routine communications. Include non-work related questions in your email check-ins, on calls and in instant messages. You could send a message like, 'Hey! This has nothing to do with work. I just wanted to know, how are you? How was your week / weekend? How are your kids?' If they resist and it feels like prying you can ease up. It's not an opportunity for you to ask every question you ever wanted to know about their life. Keep it short. The most important thing is to connect with them and let them know you care.

Something simple you can do to let the people on your team know you care about them is know when important milestones are coming up for them. Make sure to create a bit of a celebration. For example, at a meeting when it's Mimi's birthday, take the time to say, 'Everybody, it's Mimi's birthday today!'

There's freedom for you *and* the people you work with when you take the time and make the effort to connect with them on a deeper, meaningful level.

Practice Tips:

- Create structures to enable you to know your team members' goals, dreams and what matters to them. Keep asking yourself, *How can I support them in fulfilling these?*
- Intentionally create water cooler time for your team that you are

not around for.

- Include personal check-ins on a daily basis in your communication with team members.
- Celebrate milestones like birthdays, anniversaries and major life events.
- Plan regular face-to-face video calls with your team members who work remotely. Video conference team meetings are great.

Habit #15: Know what matters to your team and check in with each person daily.

No Man Or Woman Is An Island

'Make it a habit to tell people thank you. To express your appreciation, sincerely and without the expectation of anything in return. Truly appreciate those around you, and you'll soon find many others around you. Truly appreciate life, and you'll find that you have more of it.'
~ Ralph Marston, writer and publisher of *The Daily Motivator*

It's important to organize your life in a way that creates and nurtures relationships that support you and your business. Having people around you with whom you can be yourself and real opens a whole world of self-expression. Having authentic connections with people in your life creates freedom. You are free to be yourself and free to grow in ways that serve you and your business. However, entrepreneurs often find themselves working alone, isolating themselves or restricting their self-expression and that comes with inherent dangers.

One danger is, by isolating yourself, you start to have conversations with yourself. Before you know it that solo conversation is leading you down a spiral to nowhere in your own mind. You keep talking to yourself and your responses are so off base and stupid that you just climb further and further down the hole.

Habit #5, knowing your trigger behaviours, is your early warning system. For example, knowing that one of your trigger behaviors is isolating yourself gives you advance warning that you are about to go down that spiral hole if it comes up. When I know I am going down that hole I immediately get in communication with three people: My partner wherever in the world she happens to be roaming, my accountability partner and endurance coach in Utah, and finally a close friend and *Amorvita* Associate in Toronto.

I let them each know that I am I heading down the hole and what kind of support I need. If I don't need anything at that time, I'll ask them to keep an eye on me for the next few days. The important thing is having people in my life who I can tell the truth to and who I can ask for what I need when I'm not at my best.

These are the kinds of relationships we all need to have in our lives. Entrepreneurs tend to think we always have to put our best face forward. There's this pervasive phenomenon where we don't think we can actually tell the truth. We don't think we can actually say to someone, 'My cash flow sucks this month!' We won't share that we need more sales, or that it's not all rosy right now. Or that last month was great but this month is terrible! But it's in being honest about where you're at and what you're dealing with with supportive people in your life that you'll find freedom. You'll have the freedom to be honest about what's really going on, and you'll open the flow between you and the people in your life. You enable people to contribute to you, and you grow past the point you were stopped at and couldn't get past on your own.

Not only is it important to stay connected with supportive people, it's important to have *authentic relationships* with *everyone* you come into contact with. My photographer Cynthia and I were talking about this just the other day. She shared about wanting authentic relationships with her clients. I was surprised because her clients were women who were either naked or almost naked in the photo shoots. They're so vulnerable when they're with her. They're bearing all, in close proximity with nowhere to hide.

When she started as a photographer, she felt distant from her clients. She would wear blazers and suits. She thought it was OK even though she was uncomfortable. Once when she was in Chicago, she saw one of her favourite photographers speak. The photographer spoke about being honest about who you are with yourself and the people around you. She went on to say she has this really awful, hideous, loud laugh. She also tells really dirty jokes. She sings and dances and is incredibly silly. Most importantly, she lets her clients see *all* of this.

At the time, Cynthia wished she could have that freedom when she was with her clients. She wanted that same kind of relationship with them. At heart she is funny, silly and vivacious. She hid those characteristics because she felt she needed to be a certain 'professional' way. Trust to her meant a suit and not laughing. Professional meant being serious and not asking too many questions. She thought, *Don't get too personal and don't get too private.*

Cynthia shared with her mentor that sometimes on a shoot a swear word will come out of her mouth. Her mentor said, 'Go with it. It's who you are. If you honour who you are, you will create beautiful, authentic relationships with your clients.' She told her to, 'Step into the shoot like you're meeting up with your best friend. Not that you actually want your client to be your best friend, because they're hiring you. But you want to create a connection like that because you want the best outcome for both of you out of working together. If the client doesn't see a best friend, the photoshoot will get done but there will be no connection; no story. There will be nothing deeper to add to the experience of the photoshoot.'

Cynthia came home from Chicago and changed everything. She started wearing comfortable clothes. She had conversations with her clients while they were doing their makeup. She asked them questions about their lives. She started being herself and being silly.

Being herself she suddenly attracted more clients. It created warmer conversations and got her more excited to do her the work. When she went to the computer to edit photos, she wasn't just looking at an image. She was looking at a human with a name and a personality. She became attracted to their stories. The photos meant more to her because she had a much stronger connection with her clients.

She noticed other changes. There was no longer a separation in the way she would act in her business and in her personal life. Everything just sort of melted into one. Being herself with her clients pulled the dividing wall down. It gave her the freedom to just be.

Practicing this has made a huge difference for her. It gives her the opportunity to consistently have honest conversations with people. When she takes photos now, she takes care to make sure she knows a lot about her clients. It's authentic because she loves people. And she's not hiding herself anymore. For years she had apologized for being herself.

Her clients trust her because of the relationship they have with her. And interestingly, she actually feels like she is treated more professionally than before. By not being herself, she was holding back in her business. Now business conversations flow easily and clients completely trust her. They say things like, 'OK, you do this – it's entirely up to you. This is your photoshoot.' I laughed when she told me this because I'd said almost that same thing to her a week before.

Create and develop powerful, real relationships with colleagues, friends, clients and your team. You cannot even imagine the access to support that your network will provide. They are an access not only to emotional freedom but physical freedom as well. And give yourself the freedom to fully be yourself with your clients and everyone you come into contact with. You will surprise yourself at all the amazing things that show up when you practice both of these things.

Practice Tips:

- Practice telling the truth about your business. Notice when people ask, 'How are you doing?' and you lie and say 'Fine,' 'Great,' or something similar.
- Be yourself. Don't have different versions of you for your family, your friends and your business.
- Ask for support when things are not going well. Give up the idea that people will not help or that you're being a nuisance.
- Create a small team to call upon when you know you are spiralling into a hole and indulging a trigger behavior or in negative self-talk.
- Stop talking to yourself about yourself. When you do this, most of the time you don't have a lot of good things to say.

Habit #16: Create and develop powerful, real relationships with everyone you interact with.

FEATURE INTERVIEW

Evan Kosiner is a Canadian serial entrepreneur, broadcaster and philanthropist. His achievements include The Governor General of Canada's Caring Canadian Award and bringing HuffPost Live to Canada in partnership with AOL. He co-founded and now acts as Chairman of *Skate To Great* (skatetogreat.org), one of the largest skating related charities in Canada.

Evan also Directed and Co-Executive Produced a feature length film starring rapper Drake, entitled *Drake's Homecoming: The Lost Footage*. The film was covered by many articles including Rolling Stone Magazine, Billboard Magazine, TMZ and The LA Times.

He owned Radio Development Group providing over 80% of the content that aired on SiriusXM on Canada 360. Evan ran Bulb TV, the first North American channel to broadcast in 4K and 8K formats. He hosts *Entrepreneurship*, a live television show with notable guests including the founder and chairman of The Four Seasons. Evan appeared on CTV News as a business contributor.

What does entrepreneurial freedom mean to you personally?

It means getting your business to the point that it runs itself. You know you can be as involved or uninvolved as you like. For a lot of entrepreneurs that's a major step. When you get to the point that you have a team that's good enough to run operations and you can just give direction and let others do it – it's a monumental time. It's being able to delegate and have a team that you trust.

What three habits contribute the most to you achieving that freedom?

It's the same 3 characteristics I would use to qualify someone I would bring on board my team. It's someone who has intelligence, character and talent.

You are intelligent if you are bright, witty and look at things from multiple angles. Character is being quirky, charismatic and a little bit out there to the point that people are left a little bit on guard. They aren't sure which way you're going to go. There's often humour tied in and being able to connect with people on that level. Talent is almost a combination of both. It depends what area you're looking for to bring someone on board or act as an entrepreneur. These three characteristics translate into habits.

It's great to introduce people. A lot of people are passive when it comes to networking or being at an event with people. A lot of the great business people I know want to put this person and that person together when they're having a conversation. Often times, there are a couple of people that they know and a couple of people that the other person knows. They make the conversation occur in such a way that it's entertaining for others.

You need to always be looking for your own weaknesses in a way that you can be improving on things that aren't working for you. There are times I know there are things I won't do so I need to put somebody else in place or have somebody do those things. Otherwise they're just not going to get done. Be really aggressive when it comes to scheduling and writing things down. As you get busier and busier, making and more importantly reading over your notes are the only way things are going to get done. You've always got to have systems in place to be able to reflect on the things that are important to you. When you start to grow and have multiple business, it becomes so big that it gets to the point that it's bigger than your memory. Then it's about trust in your team and making sure they have the systems and structures in place so that you aren't urgently needed.

If I put someone in my calendar, I'm there for them in that period. When you are actually with someone, being with them and not getting taken away goes a long way. People notice that and pick up on that sort of thing. The old saying that, "You don't want to do business with someone who you wouldn't go for beers with," often times I find to be very true. It's about creating the comfort and the atmosphere in an authentic way. A lot of people comment about the fact that I provide hospitality and try and go that extra mile. Doing the little things that provide that personal touch. People know they can depend on you or your business.

Give us a picture window into how you start your days.

I try not to get up until 11:00 in the morning where possible. I personally like to stay up late and sleep in, it's the old DJ mentality. I'm not a morning person at all. I wake up, watch a couple of minutes of the news or see what's going on in the world on my iPad or my phone, sit down and check my emails for a bit, get ready and then go out and do errands for a while. Often times I find just going for a coffee or out for lunch lets me do a bit of a brain dump and just regroup. I consider my time at the bar when I go out drinking – it's research and development time; it's time to hang out and think about what's going on in terms of different businesses or ventures that I want to pursue and things like that. Every day is different.

What's the most important habit entrepreneurs should have?

Networking is what it boils down to. I don't mean, 'Let's go to a networking party and meet as many people as we can, get their business cards and follow up and bother them.' No one likes that. I find that to be the ugliest part of new entrepreneurs who are looking to try and meet people. No offense to them, but they are probably on the same level as the entrepreneur that is there quite often. Other entrepreneurs that are more established don't have the need to go to these things because they already know everyone that they need to get in touch with.

It's about reaching out to other businesses as a habit and networking that way. Introduce yourself to new people and target certain people that you read about that moved into a new company. Send them an email or give them a phone call. Don't bother them too much. Provide value within that email, letting them see what they are going to get out of the relationship.

The funniest thing was networking with FedEx. I cold called FedEx for the charity *Skate To Great*. We weren't registered and this was a fortune 500 company. Most of them don't deal with an unregistered charity. I had to call Adrian who was their Vice President of Marketing and he's Australian. I found it funny because he had never been on the ice. Bless the people over at FedEx, they've been so great and provided so much so we can get skates to kids across Canada. All that happened out of a cold call with someone, who has never gone skating, from Australia let alone Canada. Don't get discouraged from a couple of no's. Find out who their competition is and keep on pitching yourself to other companies or come up with a different business model. The world is your oyster.

Any final thoughts to share about entrepreneurial freedom?

You have to go into it for the ride. Be prepared for things not to work out and be prepared for things that you never thought would work out working out. Make sure that when you're going out there you are definitely providing value for other people and they see what they are going to get out of a particular venture. If they don't see merit in it and if it's not blatantly apparent, you're not going to get very far.

CHAPTER **THREE**

ASPIRE

Know Why

'The two most important days in your life are the day you were born and the day you find out why.'
~ Mark Twain, author, *The Adventures of Huckleberry Finn*

Nobody starts a business without having some form of a passionate spark – something that got them lit up. Something that had them ask themselves the right questions to want to take the big leap of courage of being an entrepreneur. Many refer to this as your *Why*. Your *Why* goes by many different names including your personal mission and purpose. No matter what you call it, being clear about it is not just important; it's critical.

Shawn Bearman is a great business coach and one of *Amorvita's* Associates. We kicked around some great ideas on this topic one afternoon. The first thing we became crystal clear on is that if you are an entrepreneur who doesn't know your *Why*, just stop. You need to stop everything you are doing in your business right now until you create this.

No one is consistently successful in business without a clear picture of *Why* they're doing what they do. You see, when a business owner is clear about their *Why*, it usually doesn't take long for a client to figure it out as well. And this is a great thing. Your clients can connect to your business when they know you're driven by a vision and purpose, especially when your purpose is bigger than you.

At *Amorvita*, we have 4 questions we ask entrepreneurs to have them begin thinking from a place of what matters to them. The last and final question is, 'Why does that really matter to you?' We ask that question again and again until the answer ends up being something like, 'Just because it does!'

The *Why* or purpose almost never has anything to do with the individual. Typically it's about creating something for the people they care about. Sometimes before we get to the real *Why*, we need to peel away all the surface layers. A common layer that usually pops up first has to do with having money or material possessions. There is almost always something underneath that's related to making a difference with others. For example, when they say, 'Money,' we dig deeper and they say something like, 'I want to be able give *x* to my family.' Or, 'Because this group needs *y*.' Or, 'Because I want to build schools in Africa.' And then when we ask more about the African schools, we find out that it actually has nothing to do with schools, but rather that it comes from a deep commitment to children having access to education.

You started your business with a spark, idea or commitment to something that's important to you. Being aware of and building and operating from that place is critical to experiencing fulfillment and freedom in your business.

When you are not operating from your *Why* or personal mission, the reverse also holds true. The moment you are experiencing struggle in your business, it's time to stop. Get clear where there is a disconnect between your current actions and your *Why*. The struggle is almost always related to some disconnect or incongruence between those two things. Take the time to find your way back to the spark that got you motivated, inspired, lit-up and passionate in the first place.

I have seen many different techniques to discover and articulate the *Why*. There is no one correct way. What's important is that you are connected to it. It needs to resonate with you to your core. My *Why*, as you might have guessed by now, is that entrepreneurs live with freedom. It's what I fight for and what I love for. It's the basis of everything I do – what drives me every single day. Nothing can shake me from it. I've put this purpose into a phrase that re-inspires me every time I see it:

> *I exist to listen to people with unconditional love and empower them to pursue their passions and achieve things that they think impossible.*

When you get your *Why* nobody can mess with you about it. I'm going to transform 1 million entrepreneurs in my lifetime to live with freedom. Everything I do, every business I run and every action is to create freedom for entrepreneurs. There is no question about it. People can ask me questions and even challenge me, but no one can shake me off my commitment. It's down in my bones. It's who I am.

And people do try to mess with me about my *Why*. When I'm at events and speaking engagements, people try to convince me about what they think the limits are or why I'm wrong. I'm polite but firm and say some version of, 'I respect your opinion. Entrepreneurs will achieve freedom out of what I do. They will pursue their passions and achieve the things they think impossible. It's just the way that's going.' People will either align with what I'm creating or not. Either way, I'm ok.

One pothole entrepreneurs get stuck in is that they want to do business with anybody and everybody. Every business owner needs to look at this: If clients are not in alignment with your *Why*, don't work with them. It will only cause you problems in the long run. It will always come back and bite you in the butt. They won't get value out of working with you. And you won't get any closer to fulfilling your mission.

It's not appropriate that every person on this planet do business with you. I interview entrepreneurs I'm thinking of working with. If it's not a fit, I'm happy to refer them to someone else. Not only might they not be aligned with my purpose, they also might not be willing to do the work needed to achieve freedom. Some entrepreneurs aren't coachable. I can teach entrepreneurs anything to have a successful business and achieve freedom. But I cannot teach someone to be willing. They're either are willing or they aren't.

When entrepreneurs work with clients who are not aligned with their *Why*, a few things consistently happen. If you look through your client list, these people will immediately jump out to you:

- There are discrepancies between what the client says they want and what their actions show.
- Basic respect and integrity are is missing in the relationship.
- They don't return calls or emails, or at least not in a timely way.
- They don't give you the information or supply what you need in order to get the job done with them.
- They don't care if they mess with your schedule.
- They don't care about the same things you care about.
- They don't pay their bills on time.

- You find yourself bending over backwards for them.
- They don't come to you directly with concerns and instead bad mouth you behind your back.

Entrepreneurs often get caught up in the sales-at-all-costs game. It's easy to do when your livelihood depends on having business. It can be hard to say 'no' to a paying client. But consider this: Imagine you owned a restaurant and your restaurant was full. One customer starts to verbally abuse another. Are you going to let him stay, hoping he buys more from you, or are you going to kick him out? Be the same way with clients who are not a match with your *Why*, regardless of what kind business you own!

Freedom lives in letting your purpose be your compass. Let your *Why* inform the decisions you make in your life and in your business.

Practice Tips:

- Schedule time right now to get clear on your Why if you don't know what it is yet.
- When you experience struggle, identify where you're acting inconsistent with your *Why*. Make immediate changes.
- Identify the clients in your business that do not align with your *Why* and fire them.
- Before accepting new clients, ask what you need to in order to determine alignment with your *Why*.
- Hire vendors and service providers who are aligned with your *Why*.

Habit #17: Get very clear on your *Why*. Share it and be completely unshakeable about it.

Create Your Destination

'Chase the vision, not the money; the money will end up following you.'
~ Tony Hsieh, CEO of *Zappos.com*

Shortly after my two-year engagement ended, I found myself inexplicably taking two steps forward and three steps back in life. Nothing made sense about why this was happening. One day it dawned on me that the future vision I had created included my ex in every aspect of my life. Everything I was doing lacked a future that was mine and the future from before had now expired.

I took a week off, left the city for a chalet up North and started to deal with my 'futureless life.' During the first couple of days up there I allowed myself the space to let go of the past and then went about creating my new future. Here's what I came home with:

The year is 2024 and I awaken to the rising Caribbean sun and can hear the sound of the rising tide on the shore. I am 56 years old but don't look a day older than 40. I'm blessed with great family genetics but that is complimented by my year-round tan and regular time in the ocean. I love living a life where I follow the sun and never need more than two layers of clothing.

I take a moment to thank God for the life I've created for myself, my family, friends and clients. I am grounded, peaceful and love-centred. It's great to be working with those closest to me and satisfying to know that Kaeleigh has the choice to do whatever she chooses. I roll over and passionately kiss the hot, young, intelligent companion who is gracing my bed this morning. She can wrap those sexy legs around me anytime! Enough distraction for now D, it's time for your workout. The New York marathon isn't going to run itself!

After my workout and breakfast on the outdoor terrace, it's time to prepare for my conference call with the 50 Amorvita Associates from around the world. I am rolling out the theme for our quarterly summit that is taking place in New York City this summer. It's all about redefining the way entrepreneurs work and live around the world. I am looking forward to my trip next month to review the advanced preparations. I get to visit with Bert and the New York Associates. God it's great not to have to fly coach anymore! Just one of the benefits I appreciate from leading a successful team and being a main stage and keynote speaker all around the world.

I think I'll pop over to my Mom's place and call down to my dive shop to see if the team can get me out to a wreck dive before Dom, Bryan, Bonnie, Mom and everyone are over tonight for dinner. I'm pretty sure I can fit it in. Time to get back to work D, you have 5 business operations managers, plus the micro enterprise investment team and the African orphan foundation Director to check in with before leaving the house.

Note to self for my forward time planning this week: Increase the Top 100 from 4 things/year to 5-6; I'm adding too many things to my list to finish them before I die! Also, schedule some more time to enjoy the toys I already have. What's the point in having a boat, plane, bike and great cars if you aren't enjoying them as much as possible you silly guy? But then again, that's a really minor thing considering I'm content, fulfilled and always challenged to create the next level to take myself and those around me to. God I love my life!

Once you're clear about why you're doing what you're doing, the next step is to create *what that will look like*. My preferred method and the one I use with clients is a 10-year vision that includes all 12 Key Areas of Life (we'll go into detail together on these areas in Chapter Four: *Love*).

There are two questions that always come up about the long-term vision:

- How far out is the right amount of time?
- How does this relate to a vision board and do they serve the same purpose?

I don't believe there is one single 'right' answer to the first question. My initial answer is that 10 years isn't the 'right' amount of time. Neither is a 5-year vision or a 15-year vision. I use 10 years not because it's the 'right' answer, but I do use it as a time marker for specific reasons. You will find other experts choose different times for different reasons and their methods are equally valid. For me, 10 years is far enough away that it becomes a vision to aspire to. It's also close enough to be able to create a plan. Longer than 10 years occurs to most people as a dream they can't wrap their heads around.

What about vision boards? Are they the same as a 10-year vision? Vision or dream boards are important. In fact, the next habit is all about *why* they're important, how to create them and how to have them be effective.

When you have a clear vision of your destination and where you're going, you don't have to make it happen or force it. It becomes your north star – the place you can look when making significant choices in your business and all the other areas of your life. Every choice you make in your life is either moving you closer to your vision or moving you further away. There are no neutral choices. Your vision becomes your compass.

For example, you don't have to get into a relationship because it's available. You can ask yourself the question, 'Does this move me toward my vision or further away from it?' Similarly, sometimes I'm presented with new business opportunities. If it doesn't forward the difference I am going to make in the world or my chosen lifestyle, it's a non-starter. It doesn't matter how potentially lucrative it is. All there is to do is stay focused on what the end game is.

Your 10-year vision is written 1st person and in the present tense. You can see that mine starts off with, *The year is 2024 and I awaken…* 2024 is happening right now and I just woke up. Writing from this perspective is powerful when you re-read it. I get chills every time I share it with someone and it's as vivid for me as it was the day I first created it. If you're not connected to your vision or it doesn't ring true you for you when you read it, you won't believe it. That defeats the purpose of creating it in the first place.

A challenge people have when creating their vision is letting go to dream and imagine. When you were a child you saw the world with wonder and nothing was impossible. I was clear I was going to be a doctor and a pilot who brought care to people who couldn't get access to it. I shut down my future as a doctor one day as an adult during one incident and with one decision. I've since created a vision with the same scope of service in an area I have come to love even more. Let yourself create your vision through the eyes of the child within you.

Practice Tips:

- Plan time to create your 10-year vision in a place that is peaceful, inspiring and creative.
- Let your vision free-flow at first. Don't edit or suppress your ideas.
- Allow your inner child to dream and imagine when creating your vision. Let out the dreams that you haven't been giving yourself permission to have.
- Include all 12 Key Areas of Life in your vision (from Chapter Four: *Love*): *Environment, Well-Being, Growth, Spirituality, Contribution, Self-Image, Business, Wealth, Social, Family, Recreation* and *Love.*
- Write in the present tense and in the first person, as if you are living your future right now.

Habit #18: Create a powerful, inspiring 10-year vision that includes all 12 Key Areas of Life.

Connect Emotionally To Your Future

'If you can dream it, you can do it.'
~ Walt Disney, entrepreneur, animator, voice actor and film producer

When you think about your goals, are they just OK? Or do you get excited, jacked up, pumped up and think, 'Yeah! Let's go! I can't wait!?' The lack of pure excitement I see too often is exactly why I added this in the *Aspire* chapter. People tend to go halfway when it comes to creating their future.

Lots of people create visions and set goals and even create visual representations of them. I see this practice often with entrepreneurs. People have different versions of this practice – some call it vision boarding, dream boarding, etc.

Creating these visual representations is only 50% of the equation. Many people miss the second, *absolutely critical* piece. The missing piece for many is that they haven't created an emotional connection with that vision board. Skip that and you miss the opportunity to engage a powerful brain system you have that helps you move toward your visions.

When you connect emotionally to something, your brain's limbic system starts to generate chemicals. Brain processes go to work subconsciously. Whether you consciously know it or not, you begin to generate actions consistent with the images on your vision board. You start to pull that future toward you.

Consider that we have both conscious and subconscious parts of our brain. The conscious mind handles voluntary thoughts, awareness, self-control and planning. Our conscious mind can overpower automatic habits. This is where willpower lives.

The subconscious mind is located in the limbic system and the brain stem. It has been around for millions of years versus a few hundred thousand for the conscious mind.[7] It's always at work without any conscious effort. It handles internal organ control, insight, creativity, emotions and entrenching and managing habits.

The subconscious is faster and more efficient than the conscious mind. While your conscious mind is resting, your subconscious is still working. It's solving problems, uncovering opportunities and comprehending the incomprehensible. It's busy building memories and prodding you to start and stop habits.

Your subconscious mind communicates with your conscious mind through your intuition and gut feelings. They let your conscious mind know your

---

[7] http://richhabits.net/understanding-the-conscious-and-the-subconscious-mind

subconscious mind figured something out that it hasn't seen yet.

No action or activity is ever pointless. Everything we do moves us forward in some way, even if it's just in learning from the experience if doing it. But, you can greatly diminish the effectiveness of creating the vision we talked about in the previous habit if you don't take the time to get emotionally connected. Save yourself the time of creating and working on things that aren't effective. Engage your limbic system and subconscious mind with your future.

How exactly do you engage emotionally with your future? Do you just stare at the vision board and get excited? Not quite. The first step happens as you create your vision board. Are you excited about the images you're choosing? Can you feel yourself there, in that future, now? Can you hear the sounds, smell the smells, and taste the tastes? Engage all your senses while you're making the board.

Then, once it's complete, sit in front of it and notice what emotions are there. If it doesn't inspire you or get you excited then it's time to make some changes. You're looking for an inspired 'butterfly feeling' in the core of your emotion centre in your chest or abdomen when you look at it.

Assuming it passes the emotional test, a good practice is to write the emotions you experience down. How do you feel when you connect to your future? Do you feel inspired or motivated? Do you want to climb to the top of a tall building and shout from the tops of the rooftops? Write all those feelings down.

There's a picture of a man (the future me) with a 'six pack' of abdominal muscles on my vision board. I've never had a pack of *anything* related to my abs. Over my lifetime, I've had four major abdominal surgeries. They collectively left over two feet of scars and weakened my core muscles. When I see the six pack on my board, I'm inspired and moved to triumph over my life circumstances and overcome the odds. It's not about vanity. It has everything to with the *Disney* quote that started this section: If I can dream it, I can achieve it.

That image motivates me to choose different foods. As I feel inspired and excited I engage my limbic system and my subconscious goes to work problem-solving. It begins creating habits that are supportive of achieving the six pack. Choosing the salad over the sub is easier. It's not matter of a good vs. bad choice. Rather it's an inspired choice because I'm connected emotionally with my future.

There's another picture on my board of a woman and I sitting in lounge chairs holding hands. We're sharing a bottle of wine and looking at the sunset. It's not me in the actual picture, but it's me every time I see the image. When I emotionally connect with that image, my heart instantly opens. I don't how else to describe it. The presence of that future, that romance and that partnership in my life *today* makes me more available today. I experience my vision going to work on my subconscious mind immediately.

I connect with my vision board every morning and at the end of every day. I know it's going to work on me at a subconscious level. That's the critical second 50% of the equation I mentioned earlier – a daily practice of stopping and getting emotionally connected to your vision board.

Often people put their vision boards on a wall, on their computers as a screen saver or on their cell phone. Pretty soon it becomes just like any other wallpaper and blends into the background. Stopping and getting emotionally connected to that board must be an intentional act.

The last thing I will say about this is that your picture choices are important. I have a picture on my board that I need to replace. It's a picture of a sailboat. One of my future commitments is to co-own a boat in the British Virgin Islands (BVI). When I first created the board I imagined a sailboat. As I talked the plan out with one of the co-owners, we realized we don't a want a sailboat. We want a catamaran. It's time to put a picture of a catamaran on my board. If I don't, what my subconscious mind will go to work on is manifesting a sailboat.

If you want a family of three kids, don't put two your board. Your limbic system and the universe will give you exactly what you are asking for. Be specific and accurate. Remember that when you engage your brain's limbic system you are actually engaging your emotion centres. They pull forth actions consistent with manifesting what's on your board. Be selective and specific so you can emotionally connect to the future you desire.

Practice Tips:

- Create your vision board from your 10-year vision. Allow the images to bring your written vision to life.
- Choose images that are a match for what you want, i.e., don't choose a sailboat if you want a catamaran.
- Have your vision board in as many places as possible, for example on the wall, on your computer, on your phone, etc.

- Plan time to intentionally connect emotionally to your vision board at least twice a day to prevent it from fading into the background.
- Use ad replacement software or apps to put images from your vision board into your browser. Instead of seeing someone's ads, take control of the images you see.

Habit #19: Create your vision board and intentionally connect to it emotionally daily.

Have A Bucket List And Live It

'It's your place in the world; it's your life. Go on and do all you can with it, and make it the life you want to live.'
~ Mae Jemison, physician and *NASA* astronaut (first African-American woman to travel in space)

Dr. Gilovich, a psychology professor at Cornell University, has been untangling the complex web of happiness for over 20 years. He discovered happiness is not sustained by buying the things we want, even when they're things we highly desire or consider to be an extension of our personality. Gilovich explains that, 'One of the enemies of happiness is adaptation. We buy things to make us happy, and we succeed. But only for a while. New things are exciting to us at first, but then we adapt to them.'[8] The novelty wears off along with the happy feelings.

Buying new items provides novelty but lacks an essential ingredient to *maintaining* happiness. Dr. Gilovich said, 'Experiences are a bigger part of ourselves than our material goods. You can really like your material stuff. You can even think that part of your identity is connected to those things. Nonetheless, they remain separate from you. In contrast, your experiences really are part of you. We are the sum total of our experiences.'[7]

His reveals what many of us know to be true. Our richest and most precious memories do not come from material goods we've purchased. Instead, they're a result of experiences we've had. You can become adapted to your new phone after using it for a while. When the novelty wears off, you'll be searching to replace it, or it won't mean anything to you anymore. Opportunities to have experiences of a lifetime cannot be replaced and

---

[8] http://www.under30experiences.com/blog/the-science-of-travel-happiness

won't be forgotten. Physical things are separate from you since you are purchasing material goods. Experiences are a *direct part of you* and become a part of defining you.

This is how a recent conversation I had went:

Damian: Why did you start your own business?

Colleague: Because I wanted to be free and have flexibility in my schedule to cause peace on the planet.

Damian: And why is having flexibility in your schedule important?

Colleague: So that I can do what I want, when I want.

Damian: Why is doing what you want, when you want important?

Colleague: Because I get to choose what I'm doing instead of someone dictating how I live my life.

Damian: And what are some of the things you want to do because you have this new-found time freedom?

Colleague: Well, I don't exactly have new-found time freedom. Not yet. But when the win comes, travelling to Israel is on my bucket list.

The Mirriam-Webster dictionary defines a bucket list as a 'List of things that one has not done before but wants to do before dying.'[9] I affectionately call mine, 'My Top 100 List.' It's now more than 100 items long and I love that I'm still adding more. Why limit myself?! So far, I've accomplished 18 out of the 117 items on the list. Writing a book was the first thing I wrote when I started the list. So it's pretty cool for me that you're reading this!

My colleague originally said she didn't believe in having a bucket list. To her it seemed like a long list of dreams that wouldn't be achieved. She's not alone! In my experience, many entrepreneurs generally frown upon a bucket list. Many of them have given up on their dreams. They doubt that they'll *actually* achieve the freedom they created their businesses to be able to experience.

Some don't remember that they have bucket list dreams until they're asked

---

[9] http://www.merriam-webster.com/dictionary/bucket%20list

questions about them. Then all of a sudden they remember their dreams. The list often appears when entrepreneurs identify *Why* they created their business – to fulfill their purpose that we explored in Habit #17. Not far behind is achieving their dreams and wishes.

Many entrepreneurs live with plans like, *Later when my business does* x, *then I will* y. For me it was: *Later when I make more money (x) then I will travel (y).* Try turning the whole sentence around and see what happens.

When you put the sentence in the reverse order: *If I promise to do* y *this year, my business will produce* x, suddenly, you can have the life that you started your business to have. Do you think my colleague would wake up differently knowing her trip to Israel is coming in the next 6 months? Not one ounce of doubt that she would!

Living from that perspective creates a shift. Now her entire life is there to be enjoyed, she is living her dreams and her business is feeding all of it. No longer is her whole focus on her business or does she have to squeeze in fun, freedom and adventure. What she wants in life is now fed by being an entrepreneur.

It's a completely different place to come from. Your business becomes the access for what you want in life and fulfilling your dreams. And along the way you get to pursue your passions.

Your bottom line is also impacted. If you are happier with how your life is going, you will be more productive and more focused during your work times. Higher productivity and focus will directly influence revenue in your business.

The first step to all of this is *creating* your bucket list. Where have you always wanted to go? What have you always wanted to do? Dream up new dreams. Revive old ones. Then plan to do 3 to 5 items on that list every year.

My list includes learning to type, mastering salsa dancing, learning to speak Spanish and bungee jumping. Some of them will take 10 seconds to complete, like bungee jumping. Others, like completing the Ironman, take longer to do. Preparing for the Ironman is taking me four years.

Planning to complete 3 to 5 items a year becomes a way of organizing your life and starts to become just *how you live*. Life becomes about accomplishing things that are magical and fulfilling. Because everybody has a different bucket list, what that looks like is different for everyone. But the experience is the same: Happiness, fulfillment and freedom. For me, climbing the highest points on each of the 7 continents is a massive undertaking. I already tackled Mount Kilimanjaro in Africa and that was no picnic. One of the 7 summits is Everest. I may decide not to summit Everest; I may decide only to do base camp. I get to say what the accomplishment is for me.

It's all about what your individual dreams are. Freedom comes from being able to have experiences we individually wish to have. The most important thing is that you have a list of what those experiences are for *you* and that you start doing them!

Practice Tips:

- Do a search on 'bucket list' to find websites that can support you with some ideas for your list.
- Plan the 3-5 items you want to do each year 2-3 years ahead to give you preparation time. You may find you can easily do more than 3 per year.
- Include bucket list images on your vision board and in the images of your ad replacement software.
- Search 'bucket list software' to find many free tools and apps to help create and store your list.
- Share your bucket list and plans with your coaches, accountability partners and support group.

Habit #20: Create your bucket list and the plan to accomplish 3-5 items per year.

Vision Without Action Is A Daydream

'You've got to eat while you dream. You've got to deliver on short-range commitments, while you develop a long-range strategy and vision and implement it. The success of doing both. Walking and chewing gum if you will. Getting it done in the short-range, and delivering a long-range plan, and executing on that.'
~ Jack Welch, retired chairman and CEO of *General Electric*, author and chemical engineer

So far the habits we've created in this chapter have developed a deep and wonderful sandbox for you to play in. Implementing them provides clarity around why you do what you do. You now know where you're going and the subconscious part of your brain is working for you in the background.

There's an old Japanese proverb that I love: 'Vision without action is a daydream. Action without vision is a nightmare.' Without action, your 10-year vision is a fantasy. Action without a plan is chaos. We're about to create a habit that so many entrepreneurs, in my experience, resist. We're going to create a plan to achieve your vision.

Later on in Chapter 5: *Structure*, we'll explore a few specific planning habits. For now we are going to start with how we turn that amazing 10-year vision of yours into reality.

Step number one is to create your 5-year plan. Starting with planning 5 years out from now works for many reasons. First of all, it's the halfway mark for the 10-year vision. Therefore, it's a great place to create milestones. It's also about as far out as we can plan in our minds without seeing the plan as a fantasy.

How you start your 5-year plan is quite simple: Ask yourself, *Given my 10-year vision, what will I need to have accomplished in 5 years to be on track?* Based on your 10-year vision your answers will be something like:

- I have x amount in bank
- My annual business revenue is x
- I have a team of x doing y amount of events per month
- I am published in x magazines per year, etc.

You want to ensure that you include all 12 Key Areas of Life (from Chapter Four: *Love*) and account for all of the items in your 10-year vision. This is not a business plan. This is a 5-year *life* plan.

When your 5-year plan is complete you'll have a clear plan of what you need to accomplish by the halfway point to your 10-year vision.

The next step is to repeat the same actions for 3 years and for 1 year to create your 3-year and 1-year plans. For the 3-year plan, ask yourself where you need to be in 3 years in order to achieve your 5-year plan. Then ask yourself the same question for your 1-year milestones: What would you need to accomplish by 1 year from now in order to be on track to achieving your 3-year plan? You now have a clear set of milestones mapped out all the way to achieving your 10-year vision.

Many entrepreneurs inadvertently plan to fail before they get started because they will not set aside *time to plan*. You need to create a clear path of where you're going. My favourite excuse is that we don't know what will change in the next 1-5 years. Everything changes. That's the nature of the world we live in. But that doesn't mean don't plan. Planning gives you a foundation from which you can deal with the inevitable obstacles, challenges and changes. With a plan, you're better prepared for not *if* change happens but rather for *when* it does.

Have you ever heard of the *Merlin Method?* Sometimes it's referred to as the *Merlin Process, Factor* or *Principle*. It teaches to start with the end goal you have in mind and work your way backward. At the end, you have a clear pathway to accomplishing that goal. 'Goals to milestones to tasks,' is the phrase that best encapsulates the *Merlin Method*. Business owners learn this process to reduce large, ambitious goals into smaller, achievable parts.

Your 10-year vision provides the goals. Then you set 5-year, 3-year and 1-year milestones. To reach your 1-year milestones, you break them down into tasks for each of the quarters and then for each week within each quarter. We'll get to the quarterly and weekly tasks in Habit #38. For now, keep your focus on the 5-, 3- and 1-year plans.

Remember to start with 5 years out. Let's say you were about to have a baby, and I said to you, 'Let's make plans for when your child is 10 years old.' That would occur to most people as a long way out. My daughter is 19. The idea of planning for her 30th birthday is well, absurd! Yet, what if I said let's make plans for when your baby is 5 years old and needs to start school? Now *those* plans seem doable. Plus, you might need to get on the waiting list for elite schools now if you want a chance at having your child attend in 5 years. Once you see how to plan for your child's future 5 years from now, it's easy to back it up to planning for when he or she is 3 years old and 1 year old. The same is true in planning your life.

Practice Tips:

- Schedule uninterrupted time to work on your 5-, 3- and 1-year plans. Listening to baroque music helps the thinking and creative process.
- Work on each of your 5-, 3- and 1-year plans on different days. Allow time between for your subconscious mind to process and go to work on problem solving.
- Once you're done the 3 plans, look at your 10-year vision. Ensure there is a clear path laid out for how you will achieve each item in your vision.

- Update your 1-year plan every year before the start of the new year. Review your 3- and 5-year plans for necessary adjustments to account for and manage new circumstances.
- Don't accept any excuses from yourself to avoid creating plans, for example, that you don't have enough time or that it's not a priority.

Habit #21: Create and maintain your 5-, 3- and 1-year life plans.

Be A Connector

'More than features [and] more than benefits, we are driven to become a member in good standing of the tribe. We want to be respected by those we aspire to connect with. We want to know what we ought to do to be part of that circle.'
~ Seth Godin, author, entrepreneur, marketer and public speaker

Are you a person who has their attention on others? Being generous is an access to having others give back to you. Social psychologists call it, 'The Law of Reciprocity.' This law says that when you do something for someone, there is a deep-rooted psychological urge for them to do something nice in return.

The Law of Reciprocity is an access to freedom as an entrepreneur. But, it's not a straight-line connection that most people see immediately. For example, if you take a day off, there is an immediate experience of freedom. That's easy to see right away. But the connection between giving and freedom takes a bit more for people to wrap their minds around.

Paul Zak is a *TED* speaker and professor at Claremont Graduate University in Southern California. He researches oxytocin. Oxytocin is a neuropeptide that affects our everyday social interactions. It regulates our ability to behave altruistically and cooperatively when we make decisions.

Zak is a pioneer in a new field of study called neuroeconomics. Through his research, he's demonstrated that oxytocin is responsible for a variety of social behaviours, including empathy, generosity and trust. He also discovered that social networking online and in person triggers the same release of oxytocin in the brain. What this means is that e-connections are interpreted in the same way by the brain as in-person connections. [10]

---

[10] ted.com/speakers/paul_zak

Zak believes most humans are biologically wired to cooperate, and that business and economics ignore the biological foundations of human reciprocity, risking loss. When oxytocin levels are high, people's generosity with strangers increases by up to 80% percent. This has important implications. Countries with higher levels of trust experience lower rates of crime and are ranked higher in terms of education. They do better economically. He says: 'Civilization is *dependent* on oxytocin. You can't live around people you don't know intimately unless you have something [in you] that says: Him I can trust, and this one I can't trust.'[9]

When I do something beneficial for someone, often they think I want something in return. Often I share resources I come across that I can't use. There's no direct personal benefit to me in doing so. Or I happen to meet people and I am just meant to give resources to them. I'm giving and not expecting anything back. A lot of people think that's weird. We live in a 'give to get' environment instead of a 'give to *give*' world.

Because it's a law, the Law of Reciprocity will inevitably kick in, and often I'm pleasantly surprised at how the generosity comes back to me. But I don't give in *order* to get something back. You'll find yourself experiencing a tremendous amount of freedom when you can give *just to give*. The rewards then become the cherry on top that will always surprise and delight you.

Often I refer or connect people to resources I use or have used. For example, Lesley Edwards in Toronto is my former dating coach. She's one of the first people I connect singles with when they tell me they can't find what they want. The work she did with me was extraordinary. I created peace and ease in my life around romantic relationships that had never existed before. She's one of my top 5 coaches I have ever worked with and I have worked with some pretty amazing coaches. When I connect people with her it's not because I want something back from them.

When you're connecting people, it's important to keep *fit* in mind. Are the people you want to connect the right fit for each other? At the same time, don't overthink or prejudge too much. I work with a lot of business coaches. Some specialize in working with new start-ups that haven't built much cash flow yet. I'm also connected with executive coaches who cost more than the start-up specialists I know. It wouldn't make sense for me to send the new cash-strapped start-ups to the high-level executive coaches. It wastes everyone's time and calls my judgment into question.

It's also important to consider matching styles. Just because someone's style doesn't match yours doesn't mean it won't fit with others. When I speak with someone in my network, I'm always listening for who their ideal client or customer avatar is. This develops me as a credible resource people can trust for valuable connections. Be someone who others want to receive connections from.

This is so important that it bears repeating: I'm not suggesting for you to be a connector so you can get something from other people. That defeats the purpose completely. And even if it didn't, that kind of sleaziness gets detected by peoples' crap detectors. Remember to honour the true nature of giving – give to *give*. As you give, people will naturally want to give back to you. Receiving alters our actual physiology and we want to give back. All cultures and societies teach about repaying debts. Receivers feel physically, psychologically and culturally indebted to the giver. But it needs to start with a genuine intention on your part to *give*.

Most people do this naturally because it's as a part of who they are. Some suppress this natural inclination. They may have misguided thoughts about being taken advantage of. But that's impossible when you are giving *just to give*. Giving to *give* is about the feeling you get when you're contributing to another. In general, we all want to make a difference. It's crazy to suppress our basic human desire to contribute.

When you take on the mindset of being a connector or a giver, something starts to show up: A support system naturally begins to form. Soon there is an environment of giving and receiving around you. People show up who want to empower you and support what's important in your life. You will never achieve freedom without having a supportive team and environment. Being a connector creates both.

Practice Tips:

- Practice being someone who gives in all areas of your life on a daily basis with no expectations of a return.
- Notice what happens to you and the feelings you experience when others give freely to you. Remember this is what it feels like when you give freely to others.
- Accept the gifts others give to you. Do not rob another of the opportunity and joy of giving.
- Make at least 5 business connections for others on a weekly basis.
- Notice when you start giving with an ulterior motive to get something back. Cut that out!

Habit #22: Connect people. Support others in fulfilling their aspirations and dreams on a daily basis.

Experience Gratitude

'Remember to celebrate milestones as you prepare for the road ahead.'
~ Nelson Mandela, anti-apartheid revolutionary, philanthropist and
President of South Africa

Many successful entrepreneurs I meet or interview start their day with gratitude. They schedule time in their calendar to stop and make sure they're being grateful. Most importantly, they're grateful not only for what we would consider 'good' experiences or things in life. Their gratitude has no limits or conditions; they're also grateful for the 'bad' moments or opportunities to learn.

Gratitude is a practice. If you are not actively participating in this habit, it can escape you entirely. I love entrepreneurial groups that support each other to spend more time in a space of gratitude. Daily reminders with *YouTube* links, articles, memes, etc. are great ways to remember this practice.

There are people everywhere for you to appreciate and say 'thank you' to. Gratitude is a state of mind; an energetic space that you adopt in the world. Although the opportunity is often missed, it's easy to appreciate something someone does as a courtesy. It's as simple as saying, 'Beth, thank you for the cup of coffee,' before moving on to the next part of your day.

A friend of mine stops when she thinks about someone. She sends them a quick text to say, 'I just wanted you to know that I was thinking about you and that I appreciate you.' It's such a great practice. When she told me this, I noticed that for the people I thought of during the day, even though I was grateful for them, I did nothing. I thought, 'Wow, wouldn't it make a difference if I did!' I started sending little messages when people crossed my mind. The responses I received back were amazing and so appreciative.

There are things both great and small to be grateful for. When I become conscious of my breathing, I become grateful that I can breathe. I take the time to say, 'I'm breathing and others are not. I'm grateful for my breath.'

Earlier today, I noticed I was taking shallow breaths. I have been anxious in the last 48 hours and doing things that are not normal for me. I cancelled my non-negotiables and have been working longer hours. My actions are jamming me up. I said to myself today, 'Dude, you're holding your breath. There's all this tension running through you. Just be thankful you can breathe. Just breathe deeply...breathe...' Getting back into a space of gratitude changed everything for me. It grounded me and I was able to refocus on what really matters. I felt the tension disappear. Some of us are always catching our breath. At the end of the day, we feel exhausted because we're rushing through the whole day. We don't have to be rushing all the time. You can interrupt the rush by switching your attention to being grateful for something as fundamental as breathing.

We often take our health for granted. There's a great Indian proverb that I was recently reminded of that says, 'A healthy person has many wishes, but the sick person has only one.' When you have the flu, all you want is that flu to go away so you can get back to life. I pinched a nerve in my back several years ago and I was in bed for a month. All I wanted was for my back to get better...nothing else. Everything else was second and really didn't matter to me at the time.

I participated in a workshop recently led by one of my former students Noel Walrond. Noel did a short exercise that I will never forget. He had us all stand up. He asked us to raise our hands into the air and wiggle our fingers. He said, 'Be grateful that you walked into this room – some couldn't have. Some people can't raise their hands over their head or see their fingers.' There is so much we take for granted in our day-to-day life that we could be grateful for.

This is an important habit for every entrepreneur to master. If you want to experience freedom, create the habit of being grateful many times per day. Don't just have it be something you only do once per day. When I'm feeling grateful, there's no room for negativity. The small irrelevant things simply don't matter in those moments.

Many people ask the question, 'How can I be grateful for the *negative* things that happen to me?' Consider that *all* experiences are opportunities to learn. When I pinched that nerve several years ago, it dropped me to the floor. I couldn't stand up, even with the help of two people. I went into shock and had to be taken to hospital by ambulance. There was not much I felt grateful for in those moments. On a scale of 1 to 10 the pain was an 11. It was the most severe pain I have ever felt.

For a month, everything from going to the bathroom to rolling over was difficult. I worked on increasing my gratitude level and I gradually found things to be grateful for including the love and support of my girlfriend. I was grateful for the friend who lent me the full DVD sets of *24* and *Lost*. I never took the health of my back for granted again. I was grateful for the opportunity to learn patience. And, things started to turn around.

Gratitude is a practice. Practice appreciating both the 'good' *and* the 'bad' moments in life.

Practice Tips:

- Start and end your day with a gratitude practice.
- Create structures in your day to remind you to practice gratitude often.
- Look for things to be grateful in all the 'bad' and 'negative' experiences in your life. Find the learning opportunity in all things.
- Take the time to say 'thank you' as often as possible to the people who cross your path.
- Let people in your life know they matter to you and that you are grateful for them.

Habit #23: Practice gratitude daily and often.

What Is Sacred Must Be Kept Secret

'The reasonable man adapts himself to the world; the unreasonable one persists in trying to adapt the world to himself. Therefore all progress depends on the unreasonable man.'
~ George Bernard Shaw, playwright and critic

For the longest time, this habit in my manuscript said 'INSERT HABIT HERE.' It was so annoying. I kept wondering when I would discover it. One day, I was speaking with Nat, my friend, accountability partner and endurance coach. I don't even remember how we got on the topic that led to it, but whatever I said launched Nat into a conversation about sharing our deep aspirational missions. Thank goodness we recorded that conversation!

I mostly just listened to what he had to say:

Sometimes I want to share personal transformative experiences with everyone. The experiences are so special and cool. But I have found that the more I speak about them, the more it diminishes the depth of the experience. I try to choose words to convey it. The power of my experience is reduced because I have associated it with all these words.

While I want to share, it doesn't work for me to share my experiences it with everyone. So I ask myself, 'Is it essential for me to share this with this person? Will it enhance their life? Will it enhance our relationship? Will it be a good thing for me if I share this with them?'

How does this tie to being an entrepreneur? I was reading a blog post by Seth Godin yesterday. The message was to be careful who you share your nascent ideas with – those brand new things you are just starting to think about. While most people want to be helpful, they'll squash the ideas because they're concerned about the pain you will feel if it doesn't work out.

There is definitely some wisdom here. If you are the person willing to take more risk and you share an idea with someone who is risk averse, it doesn't matter what the idea is. They see the world through risk aversion. They'll think, 'Oh no. That has a little bit of risk in it. I'm not interested.'

The idea could be awesome and completely doable, but not for them. When you share it, you get their viewpoint of their own limits or inability. That's a reflection of them, not of the idea. What you need is the encouragement and information to help figure out if the idea is good or not; the information to determine if you should pursue it, or on how to get it to work. It's smart to be strategic about who you share these ideas with.

Boundaries are a part of all the relationships I have in my life. I love and respect all people. I do my best to not prejudge or act on stereotypes. But I have a small core group of people that I share with. I have one group that I share emotional, dating and relationship stuff with. Another group I share spiritual stuff with, etc. I stick to those groups. While I respect everyone, not everyone has the same relationship with me. It's rare to find someone with whom you can share anything about any aspect of your life.

At the end of what Nat shared, I said, 'You just created my missing habit!' The same message came to me from many different sources within that same two-week period. I read the same Seth Godin blog Nat had talked about.[11] Then I attended a conference with speaker, Debra Poneman, who was fantastic. One of the things she shared was similar. She said, *'What is*

---

[11] sethgodin.typepad.com/seths_blog/2016/06/shields-up.html

sacred must be kept secret.'

Sharing sacred messages often gets in the way of fulfilling your mission. Some people will not understand what you share with them and they will slow you down. Your sacred messages are not for sharing.

It's not that people mean harm. I am certain most people never actually mean harm. Maybe in a small number of cases they do; sometimes people do just want to strip someone down. I give human beings the benefit of the doubt and think they want to contribute most of the time. But, sometimes they contribute from their perceptions and fears – often from their perceived ability or inability to execute the idea themselves. It has nothing to do with us or with the validity of the idea itself.

Why can't we just openly share with people all the time? There's no reason we can't when it comes to factual information about the world or how things work. But there are personal things that are deeply sacred to you, that in the early stages of formation often only make sense to you. They're things that you haven't found ways to articulate yet. These kinds of thoughts and ideas are often complex. Your words can't fully capture them well enough to share quite yet.

These experiences, ideas and thoughts are empowering when they're *yours*. You grant yourself creative freedom when you honour the sacredness of the ideas you have. If you give ownership of your ideas over to other people, then you give away some control. It's your bus to ride. If you give someone else the steering wheel for a bit, they can take you off course. It could be like you saying, 'We're on a bus,' and them saying, 'Actually, no, we're on a boat.' You say, 'I'm pretty sure it's my bus.' Then you start losing your initial clarity because you let other people take the wheel. They start creating doubt or, worse, they wreck what you started building altogether.

Instead, you will find freedom in protecting your sacred ideas and plans.

Practice Tips:

- Sacred messages are for *you* and are not for sharing with others.
- Select coaches and a small core group who can give you encouragement you need.
- Don't let others bring fears and limitations to your ideas and impede your brilliance.
- Notice when you, yourself bring your fears, concerns and limits into others' conversations. Stop immediately and acknowledge that

that's what you were doing.

- Stop trying to explain your transformational experiences to others. They are for you only.

Habit #24: Fiercely protect your sacred messages and new ideas like a mother bear protects her cubs.

FEATURE INTERVIEW

James Erdt is a speaker, author, success coach, philanthropist and the TV Host of *The DYNAMO Show*. He has been featured on CBC, CBS, *CityTV*, *MuchMusic* and many fitness publications. James is the 'Chief Architect of WOW' for *DYNAMO Entrepreneur* (dynamoentrepreneur.com), an innovative, socially responsible organization guiding visionaries, thought-leaders and game-changers.

Some of his notable awards include winning the Canadian Motivational Speaker Talent Search, nomination for Top 40 Under 40 and Canadian Personal Trainer of the Year. James is an Amazon Best Selling Author for the *DYNAMO Diaries Series*.

He's addressed over 500 live audiences and consulted for mega-brands like Nike, Skechers, Titika, GoodLife Fitness, One Health Clubs and Fitness STAR International. James has been featured at events with Jack Canfield, Brendon Burchard, Marci Shimoff, John Gray, Mark Victor Hanson, John Assaraf, Bill Walsh, James MacNeil, James Arthur Ray, Dr. Bruce Lipton, Janet Attwood, T. Harv Eker and Dr. John Demartini.

What does entrepreneurial freedom mean to you personally?

Entrepreneurs have opportunities to experience all kinds of freedom. Most people are not living the entrepreneur life and don't get the chance to enjoy that lifestyle. Entrepreneurs make decisions on their own. They don't wait for a boss to tell them what to do. They live the life of freedom consciously. We choose to live this lifestyle versus being told to do anything.

Most entrepreneurial types think of jobs as prisons. Many people are in a job and are 100% ok with it. But for entrepreneurial types that are stuck in the dead end job it's challenging. They're waiting for the day to end and are looking for plan B. They think of exit strategies the moment they get there.

What three habits contribute the most to you achieving that freedom?

One of the main habits I have had to practice, practice, practice is called focus. I thought multi-tasking was the way to go. It's not something that human beings can actually do. Our brain can only think of one thing at a time. When you multi-task, studies show you give up a slight element of time to refocus. It doesn't really make sense to go from this to that, because it's not efficient or effective. The greatest habit I have somewhat mastered is focus on focus with focus. It breaks into three categories.

#1 Freedom of money and time: Entrepreneurs have no ceiling on the limit they can make financially. We write our own pay cheques and have endless opportunities. We have the opportunity to attract more abundance into our lives. We get full compensation for our own inventions. We get a 100% of the recognition versus sharing it, unless we are on a team doing mastermind-type work. Entrepreneurs love living a fulfilling life full of excitement and joy. We do things on our own terms. We set our own goals with milestones to achieve and ultimately set our own pace – how fast or slow we want.

#2 Freedom of friendships: I like friendships to include family, co-workers or the people you are doing a project with. The more of a friend you are the more they respect you. People generally don't care until they know you care. When they know you care, they genuinely want to care about you. When they genuinely care about you, they genuinely care about your well-being. If they care about your well-being, you will care about their well-being. We are the sum of our closest relationships. That holds true in your personal and professional life. Most people say friends are just the people we hang out with. It's also the people you work with. Entrepreneurs tend to surround themselves with other inspiring movers and shakers, doers, big time game changers and people that really want to elevate the game. We want to spend time with people who respect and appreciate us and, most importantly, love us. That's the key: To surround ourselves with people who love us. Usually we love our friends. Otherwise you have an agenda. And if you have an agenda, it's not a real relationship.

#3 Freedom of purpose: We have fundamental values and morals and we usually relay those into our entrepreneurial life. In a corporate company, you basically bend your morals and values to accommodate working there to get a pay cheque. Whether you like it or not, you have no choice. As entrepreneurs, we have a choice. It's an ever evolving career that gives us the magical sense of purpose for living. We contribute, collaborate and empower people. Ultimately we empower the planet as a whole. We desire to create an impact and love to leave the earth better than we found it. Our number one job on this planet is to inspire.

Those 3 core categories shape the habit which is focus on focus with focus. The closer we stick to these 3 simple freedoms, the clearer everything gets. Our day-to-day actions and choices become more positive. Our mindset is focused and ultimately the louder our voice gets. The louder our voice gets, the more powerful we are as human beings. We embrace that power in a good way to share our voice, our story and our message. We share all the lessons we were gifted by the universe to be the guides and teachers of the next generation.

Give us a picture window into how you start your days.

I start my day with gratitude. I write down three things that I am grateful for. You want stuff to appear in your life? Whether it's material or love or abundance in any way shape or form, you best be grateful for it, because if you aren't, it simply isn't coming. The next step is to have the mindset of service. The focus is, *How can I serve today? How can I make someone in my world's life better today?* I set out to do that with one individual every day. Then I have a little list of how I run my day.

I wake-up at 5:00 AM and do cardio for 5 minutes to warm up. Then I do 40 minutes of yoga core work and stretching. I set my mind and stretch my body. Then I have cardio session #1 for half an hour. Then I switch to cardio session #2 to provide the variety that my muscles absolutely love. I do it at a slow, steady pace so I salvage my muscle fibers but burn the fat. I don't have any food calories in me so I'm only burning fat energy. Then I go for a swim from 7:00-7:15 AM and do 20-25 laps. Then I jump into the hot tub from 7:15-7:30 AM and make my way upstairs for meal #1. I eat after I've done all that training. Next, I get ready for the day between 8:00-9:00 AM. I shower and start my day. I call it the plork day – play/work. If you love what you do, you don't work a day in your life. From 9:00-11:30 AM is when I book meetings with individuals and I go into those meetings with a "what can I do for them" attitude, never "what can I get." Just watch the magic unfold. From 11:30-12:00 PM I get some energy from meal #2. Some people call it lunch, I call it meal #2.

What's the most important habit entrepreneurs should have?

Belief. Get out there and just do it. When I jump out of bed in the morning, sometimes it's difficult. All of us have had a rough night or we don't sleep well. We may not want to get into the consistency of a system, but it works. Going back to the consistency of a system is so important. When you say those 3 little words in the morning *just do it*, watch what happens when you bounce out of bed. Then you implement believing in yourself, because if we don't believe in ourselves who will?

Any final thoughts to share about entrepreneurial freedom?

I have the entrepreneurial freedom to say THANK YOU.

CHAPTER **FOUR**

LOVE

Love

'Being deeply loved by someone gives you strength, while loving someone deeply gives you courage.'
~ Lao Tzu, ancient Chinese philosopher, writer, *Tao Te Ching* and founder of philosophical *Taoism*

The Entrepreneur's 12 Key Areas of Life Definition of the Area *Love*

Love: *The existence and quality of profound, deep, romantic, affectionate, fond, passionate, exciting, mysterious and sexual feelings for someone.*

When I sat down to write about this area, I called Michael Santonato. He is The Relationship Master, a former *Amorvita* Associate and an international best-selling author. I asked him, 'How does a fulfilled romantic life contribute to experiencing or achieving freedom?'

Michael started by sharing a personal story…

> *Last night, I needed to come up with about $10,000 in 48 hours. I was struggling, talking to people and getting rejections. I had to call the last person I wanted to call. But it was someone I knew could make it happen. Jessica was right there supporting me, believing in me and telling me I could do it. Telling me no matter what, keep moving forward in the relentless pursuit of my dreams.*

While Michael was in the middle of breaking down, Jessica was picking him up. She gave him space to pour out everything he needed to. She said the words he needed to hear. He became clear that she believes in him. As a result, they have the experience of being on the journey together. It makes it easier. It can be hard when you're alone and pursuing your dreams.

I had to ask him, 'How do you think your story would look if you weren't in a relationship?'

He laughed so loud he couldn't stop himself. Then he shared...

> *That's a great question! Oh boy! Well, for starters, I might not have made that last phone call. I would have spun down into a dark hole. I don't know when I would have come out of it. It could have sabotaged the opportunity. She was physically and emotionally there. I got to be completely naked with her. With a friend, I would have been hoping they didn't think I was stupid or a loser.*

In one short story, he illustrated all of the things I believe for this area of life. It's important to have someone in your corner who you share this kind of connection with.

I was curious about his thoughts on us being predestined to be in romantic relationships. Do we need a romantic partner? Are we better when we are involved in a relationship?

To answer this, Michael asked if I knew what the #1 stimulation is for the human brain. I said I didn't know. Turns out it's another human brain. In our digital, high-tech world, we're constantly being stimulated. Yet, our #1 stimulation is, and probably will be for a long time, another person. We're social creatures and we need each other in order to thrive. Our survival is dependent on working with others.

So I thought, I understand that we need *social* relationships but what about *romantic* ones? I was waiting for a black and white answer and didn't get one. According to Michael we're better off, but that's not necessarily true for everyone. Relationships are a muscle; a skill. It takes practice and a commitment to be good at them.

Similarly, there are people in the word who are super fit. Think of the people who adorn the covers of the health and fitness magazines. They don't just get that way overnight. They're up early in the morning. They watch everything they eat. They're in the gym more hours per day than most people. It's an area of life they have mastered. It's no different in the

Key Area of *Love*. You need to put in the work and effort to get the results and benefits.

Bronnie Ware is a nurse who spent many years with people as they were passing away. She wrote a book called *The Top 5 Regrets Of The Dying*. She found that ultimately, the top 5 regrets were the same 5 things amongst all of the people she spoke to. One of them was a wish to have had the courage to express their feelings.

This is clearly an important area for everyone, not just entrepreneurs. But entrepreneurs seem to have the hardest time balancing this area and their business at the same time. So I asked Michael about tips for entrepreneurs to run thriving businesses and have great relationships at the same time.

The first tip is for entrepreneurs that are in a business maintenance rather than a growth stage. When their business is relatively stable, they have time and space to work on sustaining their relationship. These entrepreneurs should be putting time into maintaining their relationship, just as they take the time to nurture their staff. Their relationship also needs time. It needs maintenance, love, date nights, conversations before bed and ideally, sex. Lots of people leave the sex part out. People neglect it and it's one of the things that makes love, and life better.

The second tip is for entrepreneurs who have businesses that are in a growth stage. We all know what it's like when you have targets to hit, deadlines and goals. You're excited when you have momentum and things are moving. In this stage, it's too easy to let your relationship fade into the background for sometimes long periods at a time. What you need to do if your business is expanding is have a straight conversation with your partner. You might say something like, 'For the next 90 days I'm going to work on hitting this goal.' Tell your partner you're going to be busy like a crazy person working on the business. Tell them what it will mean for you, your relationship and the business if you achieve your goal. Ask for support. Let your partner know you may come home late or miss a date night. Ask your partner if he or she would be willing to support you while you reach for your dreams.

Having the conversation makes it all understood. A relationship with an understanding partner can sustain itself if you communicate and then pick up where you left off. And stay true to the timeline that you promised your partner. Don't stay overly busy in your business for too long. You can't keep that going for a year, 2 years or 5 years. If you do (and especially if you do without communicating about it!) your partner might leave you, because like all things, your relationship it needs care and maintenance.

These conversations about temporary changes in the flow of the relationship are the exception and not the rule. Sometimes people are black and white about this: They may say, 'I'm not going to give up date night,' or, 'I *have* to spend time with my partner.' Then they get resentful if their business takes them away from other things in their lives. Or, the opposite scenario is when entrepreneurs don't have structure at all. They throw themselves into their business and work 80 or 90 hours a week. They expect their partner to take it and be there sometime in the future whenever they finish what they have to do. Neither one of these scenarios turns out well.

Love is an important area of your life to nurture. Having the conversations and communicating with your partner is what makes it work.

Practice Tips:

- Make room in your life for the existence of a juicy, romantic partnership. If you are single, clear away the space necessary for someone to come into your life.
- Communicate with your partner about what you are dealing with in your business – good and bad.
- Allow you partner to support you. Allow him or her to be the wind beneath your wings on the days you're not sure how to keep going or feel like a failure.
- No one Key Area of Life is more important than another. They're all important to have equilibrium. Treat your love with the same respect and honour you give to your business.
- Create the quality and quantity of time needed to sustain your relationship (exchanging gestures of love, date nights, conversations before bed, sex, etc.).

Habit #25: Create, nurture and cherish a strong, powerful partnership with a romantic partner.

Social

'Friendship is the hardest thing in the world to explain. It's not something you learn in school. But if you haven't learned the meaning of friendship, you really haven't learned anything.'
~ Muhammad Ali, Olympic and professional boxer and activist

The Entrepreneur's 12 Key Areas of Life
Definition of the Area *Social*

Social: *The time you spend talking to, being involved with and doing activities with friends and people you like or enjoy being with.*

How does having a strong social life give an entrepreneur freedom? When you have a great social life it provides you with another source of or access to relaxation and peace.

There is one thing that I love most about my social life and social circle: When I'm connected with my friends, I am not concerned with what is or isn't going to happen in my business. I'm not concerned with the 'what ifs.' I'm just out having a good time. It opens up a level of play and creativity for me that I bring back with me when I return to my business. Sometimes when I'm spending time with my friends I even see the potential for a new project idea for the future.

My friendships are diverse. They span different age groups, ethnicities, sexual orientations, geographies and social status. They provide a wonderful, safe space to explore new ideas in a non-confrontational environment. I can always just be real with friends. There's no agenda or way I need to be or look. My friendships are a shelter from the storm of life and that alone is a big source of freedom for me.

They also act like an early warning detector. My friends pick up on when I'm 'off' faster than I do. They ask what's going with me. When my smart ass, cover-up response is, 'Nothing,' they immediately know I'm lying.

There have been times when I haven't spoken to a friend of mine for a few weeks. The when we reconnect, that friend will tell me that I sound so much better than last time we spoke. When I ask her what she means, she tells me that I was a little stressed and snappy before. When I ask why she didn't say anything sooner, she tells me that I wouldn't have been able to hear her at the time. She said she trusted that I needed to go away and get centred again. She was right. She knew exactly what was going on with me and supported me from a distance the whole way.

It's always so amazing to me that our close friends seem to be tapped right into our brains. I have a good friend who can tell just from my text messages that something's up. The 'nothing' answer doesn't work on her either. I'll usually hear that my texts have a lot going on between the lines.

I believe that I have taken more steps than the average person toward a life designed with equilibrium. But it's a journey and I definitely have a long way to go. I see many entrepreneurs working long hours and not leaving room for many other things in their life. Creating an environment that includes great friendships supports the equilibrium in your life. Friends also help you along the journey as they provide support and help you grow and become better.

Friends can't be (and shouldn't be!) ignored forever. Even if you go for a drink with a friend one day a week that's better than never going. I know many entrepreneurs who basically eat, sleep and breathe their business. Their friends are their work colleagues. They never actually leave work behind.

I consider myself fortunate to be blessed with an abundance of wonderful friendships. I can't even tell you how I came to know some of the people in my circle. I just know that we met somewhere along the way and it was for a reason. Some of my closest friends I have known since we were 3 years old in kindergarten in Guyana. There are friends in my life who I hang out with often. Then there are friends I don't see for 20 years and then when we see each other it's like we saw each other yesterday.

You need to cultivate your social circle if you want to experience freedom. You can't spend time or energy feeling guilty because you don't spend time with those you love.

Social media sometimes provides a great tool for staying connected. I get to see what friends are doing halfway around the world and feel like I'm up to date on the small stuff. Then when it's time to spend time with them, all the little details are already handled through having kept up with their lives on social media. We get to focus on the big things that we want to do and have amazing, quality time together.

Practice Tips:

- Remember: No one Key Area of Life is more important than another. Block out the time for your friendships and your social life the same way you would find space for your best client.
- Spend regular weekly time with your friends.
- When you're with your friends, be with your friends. Leave your business behind.
- Have friends in your life that you don't work with.
- Take time to express gratitude to your early warning detector friends for their contribution.

Habit #26: Set aside regular weekly time to nurture your important friendships and social relationships.

Spirituality

'I believe in God, but not as one thing – not as an old man in the sky. I believe that what people call God is something in all of us. I believe that what Jesus and Mohammed and Buddha and all the rest said was right. It's just that the translations have gone wrong.'
~ John Lennon, singer and songwriter and co-founder of *The Beatles*

The Entrepreneur's 12 Key Areas of Life
Definition of the Area *Spirituality*

Spirituality: *Your moments and practice of transcendence within the human experience where you discover and question the meaning of personal existence and attempt to place the self within a broader ontological context.*

How does having a rich spiritual practice or rich spiritual life impact entrepreneurial freedom? For some people the answer is obvious. Others think, 'I've put spirituality to the side and still managed to flourish – what does this have to do with my freedom?'

Spirituality can be a touchy subject for people. The first thing I should address is that when I speak about spirituality, it's all-inclusive. I'm talking about God, Spirit, Buddha, Yahweh, the universe, angels and whatever you personally consider spiritual beyond our human knowledge of existence.

In no way do I pass judgment on how people choose to express their individual spirituality. Someone could say, 'I'm an atheist and I don't believe in God.' I would ask them if they have any practices or beliefs that transcend their human existence. What do they think happens after death? Do they think a spirit or energy emerges? You don't have to believe in God to believe in energy.

One of the things to deal with around spirituality is that we are all energetic beings. There are conversations about the fact that 'you' are not the physical vessel we refer to as your 'body.' I can't go into depth about these conversations in the limited space we have here for this discussion. But consider: When people say someone has 'passed on,' where do they pass to? What is doing the passing? They are talking about the spirit or energy and not about the physical body.

I think a lot of people grapple with the fact that we are all energy. I always see skeptical faces when this comes up. Stop wondering about this; it's indisputable. What people don't deal with is that they don't see the world as it is.

When I look at my hand, what I see is solid flesh over bone, muscles, tendons, etc. That's not the whole story of what's there. In reality, my hand is made up of millions of molecules. To the naked eye, the surface of my hand looks relatively smooth. Under magnification, we can see it's not smooth at all. Zoom in further with an electron microscope and we can see the actual molecules. If we could look inside the molecules we would see the electrons and protons. They're vibrating at high speed and that's all there is. Every living or inanimate object is vibrating energy.

Whatever you are sitting on right now is vibrating energy. The wall closest to you is vibrating energy. Your entire body is vibrating energy. We forget that fundamentally we are all connected to everything around us. We are made of energy and so is everything else.

What does this all have to do with spirituality? In physics, the Law of Conservation of Energy states that the total energy of an isolated system cannot change. It is said to be conserved over time. Energy can be neither created nor destroyed, but can change form. So when I die, where does my energy go? That's something to ponder.

I have a personal perspective on spirituality and organized religion. I was raised Roman Catholic and am not practising. My spiritual practice includes reading the Torah, the NIV version of the Bible and Quran. I also study Buddhist teachings and meditate.

This may get me into some spiritual controversy. But, I believe we're laughable when it comes to this area of our lives. I recently saw a video on *Facebook* that started with Earth. Then it progressively zoomed out to our sun, other suns, our galaxy, etc. From our perspective, the earth is pretty big. Just consider how you would feel if I asked you to walk the circumference. But when the video finished zooming out, Earth was a pinprick on the fabric of the universe. Us as individuals on the planet are a pinprick on a pinprick. We are completely insignificant in the bigger scope of things. Yet each of us is an absolute miracle.

Let's say we believe that when our body dies our energy passes on and we transcend this world. Many spiritual teachings believe that our energy or spirit joins a higher power. For some reason, I always imagine this higher power having coffee with a group in the afterlife. There's a Rabbi, an Imam, a priest, a Buddhist practitioner, and a few more spiritual leaders. They're sitting around looking down on Earth laughing their butts off. They find it funny that we argue about what interpretation of the higher power is correct; that we start wars over if he/she/it takes a Christian form, a Muslim form or something else. What difference does it make? You're a pinprick on a pinprick on a freckle of the universe. It doesn't matter.

When I got to this realization, I thought, *What do I do with this now?* One day I discovered an answer whilst praying. I said to myself, *Let me consider this relationship to the higher power as a child to a father or mother. The only thing for me to do is to live my life in a way that my parent would be proud of me.* I decided that that's what matters.

Back to: What does this whole spiritual conversation have to do with entrepreneurial freedom? I believe you need to have a good relationship with your spirituality to have a shot at being free. It doesn't matter what path you choose, but rather that you choose one and that you're grounded in that choice.

Being grounded spiritually puts you in touch with yourself and with what matters. It takes away all the crap, the noise and all the 'I have to's. Only *you* get to say what would have your higher power be proud of you. That right does not belong to any institution or individual.

You will surprised at the increased feeling of freedom you will experience as you begin to implement personally meaningful spiritual practices into your days.

Practice Tips:

- Resolve anything unresolved for you in your spiritual past., for example, if there is something incomplete for you about your religious upbringing.
- Choose your spiritual practice and plan regular time to take actions consistent with it.
- Be tolerant and accepting of other people's spiritual choices.
- Do regular check-ins to ask yourself if you are grounded spiritually. Immediately resolve the issues if the answer is 'no.'
- Practice connecting to others and the environment around you as other sources of energy.

Habit #27: Have a regular spiritual practice that provides a space for you to be grounded.

Well-Being

'How would your life be different if...you were conscious about the food you ate, the people you surround yourself with and the media you watch, listen to, or read? Let today be the day...you pay attention to what you feed your mind, your body, and your life. Create a nourishing environment conducive to your growth and well-being, today.'
~ Steve Maraboli, speaker, bestselling author and behavioral science academic

The Entrepreneur's 12 Key Areas of Life
Definition of the Area *Well-Being*

Well-Being: *The general condition of your body, mind and spirit being happy, healthy and prosperous and free from disease, pain and stress.*

Well-being is incredibly important for entrepreneurs if they want to create freedom and the kind of life they desire. We get deeper into other habits in the final chapter, *Structure*, to support this even more. For now, we're going to deal with the *commitment* and *mindset* needed in order to have power in this Key Area of Life.

My endurance coach, Nat, shared a quote with me: 'Radical performance demands radical self-care.' There is so much truth to this. If you want radical physical, intellectual and emotional performance you need to practice great self-care. That's what well-being is all about.

Being an entrepreneur means being someone who takes risks. In some way, you're doing something that has never been done before. It could be that no one has run your kind of business before. Maybe no one in your family or group of friends has ever started a business. When you take up a new challenge, you need a high level of performance.

As an entrepreneur, you are usually responsible for almost everything in your business. An employee's performance in a large company can fluctuate and the company will be fine. But when an entrepreneur has ups and downs in a small business, the performance of the business usually follows suit. The ability to sustain high-level performance over a long period of time is critical.

Entrepreneurs are people willing to try many things, knowing that only one or two may work. This takes emotional maturity. The same maturity is called upon to keep our well-being at a consistent level. There is much natural, inherent change in a small business. Life becomes challenging if there is also that much variation in the other areas of life. Your physical, mental and emotional stability is imperative.

There is an increasing trend toward CEO's of Fortune 500 companies taking up endurance sports. Executive responsibilities mirror endurance performance. Executives look at the big picture performance of a business. They track numbers and look at what works, and are committed to incremental growth. Similarly, an endurance athlete learns techniques, gathers data and finds trends in long-term performance.

Participating in endurance training can teach you a lot about not making excuses. If you're not running well one day, there isn't anywhere to cast blame. Saying, 'I'm responsible' and not making excuses builds emotional and mental strength. That strength is directly applicable to your business. It could sound like, 'My job is to have this business grow. How do I manage this with no blame or excuses?' I've noticed a big shift in my own mental, emotional and physical states as a result of my physical endurance training.

Many people think Fortune 500 CEO's don't have time for an endurance training commitment. Talking about this begs the question, where are they taking the time from their 168 hours for sport? This type of training is not

15 minutes running on the treadmill 3 times a week. It's often a daily commitment of an hour or more. If they're willing to make the time in their schedules, they must be getting a significant return on their investment.

There is so much teaching out there that says that an entrepreneur needs to be married to their company. Sure, the focus investment needs to be high. You've got to be committed. You have to get uncomfortable and work hard. But you also need to work smart. Working past a certain point—overworking yourself consistently—is detrimental for you and your business. It's not smart to be working on the business for 12-16 hours a day. This doesn't lead to freedom. Quite the opposite – it's destructive.

Your body needs to be nourished and taken care of. When the well-being basics are healthy, you have a shot at radical performance. If you want to perform in business, you need to be a healthy person. You need to be able to think straight and work efficiently. Daily time to care for your well-being is critical to achieving freedom.

You might say to yourself, *A 2 hour run is so much time out of my week and I can't spare the time.* But in addition to the physical benefits, here's the magic of taking that break and getting your body moving: Perhaps in the middle of the run, while not even thinking about the business you have a moment of clarity. You have a revelation about your business – one that's smarter and clearer than if you had sat down for those same 2 hours and forced your way through research and analysis. You might have had the same moment of clarity while attending a yoga class or meditating. Too many people simply push too hard to force mental clarity. Give your mind the space it needs to be wise. Tend to your overall well-being.

Practice Tips:

- Step out of your comfort zone and current habits and take on radical self-care.
- Give your body and mind the space they need to be wise on a regular basis.
- Work smarter. Play a game with yourself to get more done in less time.
- Stop listening to the bad advice that you need to be married to your business.
- Listen to your body and what it's telling you it needs to be well. Give it what it is asking for.

Habit #28: Do something every day that contributes positively to your state of well-being.

Self-Image

'The person we believe ourselves to be will always act in a manner consistent with our self-image.'
~ Brian Tracy, speaker, author and consultant

The Entrepreneur's 12 Key Areas of Life
Definition of the Area *Self-Image*

Self-Image: *The idea, conception, or mental image that you have of yourself, including an assessment of your qualities, abilities, appearance and personal worth.*

If you don't have a strong positive self-image then the way you see and relate to yourself is restricted. As result, you diminish your ability to experience freedom as an entrepreneur.

Perfectionism is something that has challenged me on my personal journey. It has a big detrimental effect on my perception of myself when it shows its ugly head. I don't love the word 'perfectionist.' For me it's a particular kind of behaviour more than a quality, and it's a behavior that I know I am prone to act out. I always want to see things perfect before I move forward. When working on a project, the drive is strong to make every single thing the best it can be before I'll approve it.

It takes a concentrated effort on my part to let go of the notion of perfection. In 2014, this was the main focus of my personal growth and development. My theme for the year was, 'Progress Not Perfection.' Now I have a perfection red flag as one of my Trigger Behaviours. It's #16 on the list: *Am I trying to get something perfect rather than to 90% and launching it?*

For me the challenge with embracing progress over perfection was an unwillingness to accept failure. Failure was personal and it meant, 'I have failed' or, 'There's something wrong with me.' That's what the negative self-talk in my head was saying. Even though in those moments my opinions about my abilities and personal worth were two degrees north of useless, I despised failure back then so much that I would do anything possible to avoid it. This included doing things that were detrimental to me and to the business.

As human beings we find countless ways to deprecate ourselves. I wonder how the world would look if people stopped talking negatively about themselves. And what if we only listened to the positive ways in which others regards us?

Creating and maintaining a strong and positive self-image is critical for entrepreneurs. Often, *you* are the face of your product or service. In some cases *you are* the product or service. You are also where your team looks to lead by example and create the pathway. You are where your prospects look when deciding if they want to do business with your company.

One challenge entrepreneurs have with creating strength in this area is they often have an aversion to asking for support. They can think requesting help makes them appear weak or incompetent. I am not exempt from this. My first thought when I'm in a low place is never, *Who should I call?* It's the opposite. The conversation I have with myself is more like, *How fast can I fix this before somebody finds out how big of an idiot I am?*

I cannot count how many times private clients disappear without communicating. They re-emerge with some problem they were trying to get resolved on their own. The crazy thing is, nine times out of ten, a short conversation has them back on track. They almost always end up saying, 'I should have called you sooner!'

If we try to do all of our growing by ourselves, our experience of being free is diminished. Achieving the kind of freedom we want as entrepreneurs becomes harder to reach when we isolate ourselves. There's a rule I follow when I scuba dive that says never go scuba diving alone. We should apply that rule to doing self-image work on ourselves.

This does not negate the amazing results produced through meditation, spiritual practice and other solo growth activities. But at some point, even the most enlightened reach a limit where isolated self-help is no longer effective.

Entrepreneurs should have at least one coaching resource do mindset work with. It's natural that anyone you talk with when you have a low self-image moment will want to help and offer support. Remember when we discussed in Habit #24 the importance of protecting your sacred ideas and choosing who you share them with; you will need to exercise the same care when selecting who you turn to for support in this Key Area of Life.

Be careful that your coach doesn't bring their own fears or limitations to the conversation. They may try saying all the right things to make you feel better, all while completely missing what's really going on beneath the surface.

Specialists trained to work on mindset are a critical part of your support structure. A coaching colleague and former therapist recently reminded me of an important point: No amount of work on the structures in your business will make any difference if the underlying mindset issues are unaddressed.

I did a lot of work to finally get that failure is not about me. Failure is an opportunity for me, and all, to learn and move forward. When inventing a working light bulb and being unsuccessful the first 10,000 times, Thomas Edison said, 'I have not failed. I've just found 10,000 ways that don't work.' Imagine if he had stopped at 5,000, how different our world might be today. Where do *you* stop before you find 10,000 ways that don't work? Where do you diminish your self-image instead of making an unsuccessful attempt at something a great learning experience?

It's much harder to achieve something when you're telling yourself that you're no good. You need to love yourself along the entrepreneurial path if you want to have the freedom you originally envisioned for yourself as an entrepreneur. Just get out there and play! Life is not meant to be taken so seriously. You're never going to get out of here alive anyway!

Practice Tips:

- Stop giving yourself permission to speak to yourself in ways you would never speak to others.
- Don't isolate yourself! Ask for help or support when you find yourself talking to yourself in a non-supportive way.
- Keep away from well-intentioned, do-gooders who aren't actually able to help you when you have a self-image crisis.
- Rely on trained support and coaching resources who have experience working with people on their mindset.
- Learn to see EVERY 'failure' as a learning opportunity that means nothing about *you*.

Habit #29: Take actions to alter your self-talk when you start conversations to diminish your greatness.

Environment

'The first step toward success is taken when you refuse to be a captive of the environment in which you first find yourself.'
~Mark Caine, writer

The Entrepreneur's 12 Key Areas of Life
Definition of the Area *Environment*

Environment: *The conditions and influences that surround you at home and work that impact your growth, health and progress.*

We are affected by both our home and work environmental conditions that surround us. For some entrepreneurs, their work and home environments are separate locations. Others work from home or from whatever space they choose. It could be their dining room table, a desk or a coffee shop table. Regardless of where you work, it's important that it's in an environment that contributes to your freedom versus detracting from it.

I work at a minimalist-style desk. The width is about the size of 3 laptops side by side and I use a kneeling chair. Up until about 2 weeks ago there was so much stuff on the desk that I couldn't work there. I would end up relocating myself from my desk to work in different places. Sometimes I would leave my apartment to work at a nearby coffee shop. Other days I would work hunched over on my couch. When I do that, it doesn't take too long before my back starts to hurt. Are you starting to see the connection between environment and the experience of freedom?

Our environment is just as much a determinant of what we have within us to perform as food is to our biology and health. When I work at that couch my back hurts. When my back hurts I don't work effectively. Perhaps I need to take extra breaks or I am preoccupied with pain. It impacts my mood. I become irritable and annoyed; annoyed with the pain and annoyed with myself that I can't use my desk. Then comes the slippery slope. Soon I'm engaging in negative self-talk about the fact that I can't keep a small desk clean.

Being a successful entrepreneur depends on your ability to perform in your business. There's a significant difference between working at a desk with lots of papers on it and one that is orderly. And, there's a significant impact on you of working at a messy desk: The sounds we hear and colours we see all trigger conscious and subconscious responses. As human beings we're wired to collect environmental data to let us know if we are safe, if we need to be on the prowl and if food is available. This is all part of our survival mechanism. Our brains automatically create meaning that affects our behaviours and emotions. Stimuli from the messy desk sends the signal that there is crap sitting there that hasn't been taken care of. If you're like me that starts an internal conversation that I'm a slob and irresponsible.

The antithesis of freedom is captivity and having minimal control. The meanings we create from external stimuli fall somewhere along the freedom captivity spectrum. At one end are the interpretations: 'I am free and have chosen this,' 'I love this,' 'This supports my life,' 'I have control,' etc. At the captivity end are interpretations like: 'I'm tolerating this,' 'I'm putting up with this,' 'I'm a slob,' etc. These interpretations affect your self-image and therefore the level of productivity and the quality of work you do.

It's also very important that you feel good about the tools in your work environment. You may hate your home office because you have an old computer that keeps crashing. It makes it hard for you to be productive. It has an impact on your experience of your life and business. Over time, you may start to feel trapped and helpless when you walk into your office. Then you upgrade the computer. Now your environment is set up to support you to work efficiently and quickly. Your experience in your work environment quickly changes to one of joy and expansion. You take that joy and expansion into your business.

Entrepreneurs often leave tending to their environment a low priority item. But what about the daily impact it has on your ability to enhance freedom and performance in your life and in your business? Your environment is not just an afterthought or a nice thing to have. It's a critical part of you designing your life to support you in being the best business owner possible.

Stop right now and take a look at the environment you're operating in. Is your work environment supporting the flow of positive energy? Is it inspiring to you? Is it a space where you feel happy and drawn to work? Now look at the other environments in your life. Does your bedroom inspire relaxing and calming energy that supports restful sleep? Is your kitchen set up to promote vitality and health in order to help you take in the necessary fuel you need?

If your environments don't match what you want your spaces to create, it's time to make changes. Delaying action demonstrates a willingness to accept detrimental influences. Consider that you tolerate detrimental emotional, physical and mental inputs in your business and life.

When making changes in your environment, trust yourself to create what's best for you. You could try using a practice like Feng Shui to create an environment for positive energy flow. You can enlist the help of someone who is an expert in this area. The key is to do what works best for you.

I discovered a new perspective recently from the Einstein quote: 'If a cluttered desk is a sign of a cluttered mind, then what is an empty desk?' For years, I read that quote to mean that creative people have clutter and mess around them and that that's ok. Or, you could interpret that what Einstein is saying is, if an empty desk is a sign of an empty mind, it's a great starting place to have freedom to create whatever the heck you want!

What does it take to create freedom and a functional work environment? It includes functional tools that you like and enjoy using. If you have a stationary pad, make sure you like the colour and that the lines are the right thickness. You may even have your name on it. In your drawer you have a pen that you know works and you love writing with it. You have all the tools you need to create with and no clutter. You don't have 12 broken pencils and a stapler that doesn't work. You have a lot of empty space where it's easy to work and create.

Practice Tips:

- De-clutter the work environment that you identify as your desk. Create a space that invites creativity and productivity.
- Remove all of the broken and unnecessary items from your work environment. Upgrade your tools.
- Assess your home and work environments to make sure they support your purpose and the goals you're working toward. Where they aren't, stop and make immediate changes.
- Hire a professional to organize your environments if this is not something you love doing.
- When you feel trapped or confined, check your immediate environment for contributing factors. Refer to Habit #10 for additional tips.

Habit #30: Refuse to tolerate environments that do not deliver spaces of freedom and creativity. Stop and make immediate changes.

Family

> *'Family is the most important thing in the world.'*
> ~ Diana, Princess of Wales

The Entrepreneur's 12 Key Areas of Life
Definition of the Area *Family*

Family: *The quality of your relationships with the group of people who you are related to by blood, law or marriage including spouses, common law partners, parents, children, uncles, aunts, cousins and in-laws.*

A good friend of mine got into business as an entrepreneur for two reasons: The first was to be able to do whatever she wanted when she wanted with her time. This is a common motivation that I hear quite often from entrepreneurs. Her second reason was to have the freedom to be able to be available for her parents.

She isn't yet married and knows that marriage is in her future. But right now, her parents are her core family. When her 84-year-old father needs to travel somewhere, she needs to be able to go with him. Her and her family are not comfortable with him traveling by himself. Similarly, when her parents have a doctor's appointment, she needs to be there so she can ask the tough questions like, 'What are you doing and how are you going to fix my mommy and my daddy?' She knows she needs to be there for that.

A regular 9 to 5 job does not provide that freedom. In a corporate environment you have a specific number of sick days and time for vacation. Some more progressive organizations grant extra family days to be used as needed. If you need to deal with a serious illness in your family, those allocated days run out fast. Not too long ago, my family lived through the final days of my uncle's long-term fight with cancer. He was a strong fighter and lasted longer in palliative care than expected. What do families do when they run out of time off work in a situation like this? I was thankful to have the flexibility and freedom as an entrepreneur when it was needed.

My story and my friend's story are two examples of how important it is to have the freedom as an entrepreneur to make family a priority. The reverse is equally important: Making family a priority so you can have the freedom you want as an entrepreneur.

Have you ever noticed that there's an effect on your business when things are out with your spouse, siblings or parents? Somehow the issues have a way of finding their way into your life and often your work. It could be by way of extra phone calls during your workday to deal with a situation. Sometimes you're so angry that you can't work productively. You might start getting headaches, stomach aches or anxiety which affects your ability to focus on your work. The absence of long-term family peace eventually shows up in your well-being as unwanted symptoms and problems in your business.

This is often the Key Area of Life that is the first to get ignored or sacrificed in the name of business needs. The long hours needed for a new business or critical growth can be steep. We've already looked at the types of conversations that can make a difference in Habit #25, *Love*. These types of conversations also apply to your children, parents and other family members. Don't make the mistake of ignoring family issues and expect everything to be fine when you 'get around to it.'

Sometimes, your family can't relate to you being an entrepreneur. They may lack entrepreneurial life experience. Some have always held a corporate job. Maybe *their* parents held a corporate job and so did *their* parents. They don't identify with the unpredictable nature that sometimes comes with running your business, or the demands. They don't understand that sometimes you're the cook, server, busboy *and* the dishwasher.

Having family support to be an entrepreneur is not their responsibility. It's yours. Expecting them to 'just understand' or 'get it' will never deliver the kind of freedom you want in your life. You can create and be responsible for harmonious family relationships. Or, you will deal with the constant distraction and effect that dis-harmonious relationships have on your experience of freedom.

For most of us, something related to family comes up when we define what freedom means to us. For our family, having freedom can be as simple as being available to take my parents to the doctors when needed. For me, it also means my daughter Kaeleigh has the freedom to choose whatever she wants to do with her life. I want my financial plan and structures to include my immediate family as I relocate around the world. Wherever possible I want them to partner with me in my businesses.

Look for yourself and determine what is important to you in this area. How do you want to include your family in your personal expression of freedom?

Practice Tips:

- Plan weekly family time in your calendar to do things that you all love to do together or that they love to do.
- Do not tolerate any unresolved family issues or relationships in your life.
- Get professional counseling or coaching for any relationship you can't resolve within three conversations.
- Take the time to ask your family for what you need from them to support your business. Don't assume they will just get it!
- Make family time a priority in your life and heed Princess Diana's quote at the beginning of this habit.

Habit #31: Schedule a weekly time to identify any family relationships that have something 'off.' Take immediate action to get whatever it is it resolved.

Recreation

'Our age has become so mechanical that this has also affected our recreation. People have gotten used to sitting down and watching a movie, a ball game [or] a television set. It may be good once in a while, but it certainly is not good all the time. Our own faculties, our imagination, our memory, the ability to do things with our mind and our hands – they need to be exercised. If we become too passive, we get dissatisfied.'
~ Maria von Trapp, stepmother and matriarch of *The Trapp Family Singers*

The Entrepreneur's 12 Key Areas of Life
Definition of the Area *Recreation*

Recreation: *The activities you engage in to refresh your mind and body that provide fun, enjoyment, stimulation, amusement or pleasure when you are not working.*

In my experience, this area is another one of the first to go when an entrepreneur starts to face crunch time. The descent starts something like, 'I have to focus on…' or 'I have to make x happen,' etc. The sentence ends with something like, '…so I don't have time to go to the movies,' or '…so I don't have time for the party tonight.'

You can already hear the lack of freedom in: 'I don't have time.' Take a look at the unexpressed emotions between the lines: *I'm enslaved by something that I chose.* Or, I *hate the way this is going, because now I'm thinking that I have to cancel doing the things that I love.* That's a long way of saying, *I have removed permission to do the things I love.* That is self-imposed captivity and certainly not freedom.

To get my recreation time in, I do Tuesday movie night every week. I love going with someone and sharing about it with them afterward. But if no one is free to join me, I'm still going to the movies. It's something I love to do, period.

You want to make sure you space your recreation time in a way that enhances your business; not that takes away from it. There are some Tuesdays that I shouldn't go to the movies. A few weeks ago I went and it was the wrong choice. I had been at a conference for three days. I didn't plan my decompression afterward so I could have some down time and get caught up. I hadn't planned well. By the time I had to leave my place for the movie, there was still urgent, unfinished work.

I didn't enjoy the movie at all. By the end, all I was thinking was, 'I need to find a way to get all those things done in the next two days and I don't have time to do them all. I should have stayed home tonight.' There was no experience of freedom because I had trapped myself. Choosing recreational moments at all costs is not the path. Make sure you're planning them at the right times.

Planning recreation time to provide refreshment for the body, mind and spirit is essential. I recently created a list of 50 things that make me happy. I always make sure that I have at least one of those 50 items planned every week, and I plan each from a few weeks out. It's satisfying to look ahead in my calendar and see them already in there.

There are three ways to go about taking recreation time and which one you choose can make or break everything. The first way of doing it is to wait until you get so agitated with your work that you go binge for 2-3 hours on Netflix (which I have been known to do). You effectively take the same amount of time out of your week as you would watching a film. But the experience is different because you are trying to enjoy Netflix and you can't.

You can't because at the same time, you're telling yourself, *I'm avoiding. I'm using this as an escape. I'm not being responsible. I don't like that I'm doing this, or, I haven't earned this.* You're holding yourself hostage and it's a mess.

The second way of doing it is to plan it like you're going to the movies on Tuesday nights and you do it no matter what. You're clear that you work hard during the week and it's something you have to look forward to. It's something you do to treat yourself. It's fun and good for you to have something creative—and not business related—to free your mind. But you go at all costs, sometimes putting you behind in important, urgent work.

Obviously, neither the first nor second way of going about taking recreation time works, and neither earn you freedom. The third way to take recreation time (the way that works!) is to have some structure to it – plan it ahead of time. Know what you're going to do and when. Then do it as planned. But, be wise; if the recreation time arrives and you know you have urgent things to work on in your business, don't force yourself to go. Follow your instincts. What is the most important thing for you to do with that time? Just make sure you *reschedule* that recreation time; don't just skip it.

There's also an extra benefit of planning ahead. The research process and anticipation before a vacation is actually more beneficial than the actual time off. A study, published in the *Journal of Applied Research in Quality of Life*, showed that the largest boost in happiness comes from the simple act of planning a vacation. In the study, the effect of vacation anticipation boosted happiness for eight weeks.[12]

By now, you're probably not questioning the benefits of spending time on recreation. Those are probably clear. Instead, the big question about creating equilibrium in all 12 Key Areas of Life is usually, 'How do I fit it all in?' The good news is that this area can be the easiest one to do if you're willing to be creative.

You can combine Recreation with many of the Key Areas we've already discussed and even the ones we haven't. Activities in the areas of *Love, Social, Spirituality* and *Family* often involve other people. And if you do most of your activities related to *Well-Being* on your own, it doesn't take much to start including someone else.

Last week, I found myself faced with the dilemma to go to the movies or do work again! I made the choice to get the work done and moved my

---

[12] link.springer.com/article/10.1007%2Fs11482-009-9091-9

movie night to Thursday. I still got my movie *and* I got my work done. Now I have the flexibility and the freedom to do the thing I love to do when I want to do it – when it *enhances* my business. I will not be the one who says I don't have time to go because I'm too busy with work. Sometimes I see a show in the middle of the day. I get a touch more joy when I know that the rest of the world is working!

Practice Tips:

- Combine your recreation time with actions you are taking in the other Key Areas of Life.
- Don't use recreation activities as an escape or avoidance tool. Be flexible and have them *enhance*, not take away from, your business.
- Schedule recreation activities weeks in advance and get the positive benefits associated with the anticipation of their arrival.
- Plan and book your vacation time 3-6 months in advance.
- Include recreation activities that refresh your body, mind and spirit.

Habit #32: Make a list of 50 things that make you happy and do at least one of them every week.

Growth

'Most people never run far enough on the first wind to find out they've got a second. Give your dreams all you've got, and you'll be amazed at the energy that comes out of you.'
~William James, philosopher and psychologist (Father of American psychology) and physician

The Entrepreneur's 12 Key Areas of Life
Definition of the Area *Growth*

Growth: *The activities you are undertaking that improve your self-knowledge and identity, develop your talents and potential, build human capital and employability, enhance your quality of life and contribute to the realization of your dreams and aspirations.*

The entire first chapter, *Grow*, and Habits #1-8 gave you a solid start in this Key Area of Life. That you are reading this book and have gotten this far suggests you have a commitment to this area. And, all of the habits in this

126

book involve growth in some way. If you were only to take on one of the habits in this book you'd be engaging in Growth activities. This section focuses on what happens to freedom when you *don't* put attention or focus on growing.

As human beings we are more than the areas of our lives or what we do. We are complex multi-layered organisms. In the absence of growth, there is a stronger emergence and dominance of our 'identity' – our self-limiting beliefs based primarily on our past experiences.

When you invest all your time growing your business it starts to become your identity. That's dangerous! There are the obvious burnout concerns because living that way is unsustainable. But additionally, you run the risk of losing yourself (the real you) in the business. If the business fails, you fail.

I know this experience firsthand. One of my earlier businesses was called *Social Scene*. It was a unique concept in the single adult market long before the advent of *Tinder*. The business failed when I made a critical error. A legal battle consumed all of the seed capital. That drove me straight into depression. I was terrified. I went from national television features to avoiding calls and hiding from the world. I was so embarrassed to say I made a mistake that had cost my partners and the company. Most detrimentally, I lost my own identity when the business failed.

In retrospect, there were ways to turn that business around and salvage it. But my identity was so wrapped up in the business failure, I couldn't see straight. I was the business and the business was me. It was all I worked on with little or no attention given to my other Key Areas of Life. I spent my social time with work colleagues and clients. I was in a romantic relationship with someone related to the business. The situation was pretty much the antithesis of everything you've learned so far in this book. I learned the hard way that I had to make changes, fast.

What I learned is: If you're not growing you're shrinking. Your life and your business never stay the same. Think of it the same way your muscles work: If you don't use your muscles, they atrophy and get weaker. Your human potential operates from a similar place of 'use it or lose it.' Like your muscles, you need to exercise your mind, body and spirit. Working at one level will have you stay at that same level. When you push yourself to operate at a higher level, you begin to grow.

Growth activities come in all sorts of types and practices. A growth activity for one person is not necessarily a growth activity for another. People can also have different ways of taking on their growth activities.

I have a planner-type personality and need to have a structure to manage this particular area of life. Some people need a structure like I do. If you like structure, you could set reminders in your calendar or set up something you commit to on a regular basis. Some need the freedom to read, meditate or go for a walk when they feel they need it. It's easy to feel guilty in our culture. There's a prevailing attitude that if you're an entrepreneur you should be making sales call all day long. That it doesn't matter if your favourite yoga class is at 11:00 am during business hours.

It's so easy to forget that the business won't thrive if you're not grounded.

Don't have your identity become your business. You are so much more. The more cultivated, diverse of a human being you are, the more value you bring to your clients.

Today I would deal with the same situation I had in my previous business, differently. I am no longer defined by my business. It doesn't make me who I am. About a year ago I faced the real possibility that I might have to shut down *Amorvita*. I was managing a health issue and couldn't work for 4 months. I was actually amazed at how fast I sorted out that I was not my business. The business could fail but *I* was not a failure. I was clear that I could close the doors and it wouldn't mean anything about me. I would find another way the next day to make the difference in the lives of entrepreneurs that I'm committed to.

One structure I took on recently was taking a non-negotiable meditation break in the middle of my day. I now stop everything and I meditate for 10-15 minutes. It is one of the most beneficial practices that I have ever taken on. It supports my growth and has the added benefit of supporting me spiritually. I'm a whole new person heading into the afternoon.

It's counter-intuitive given what our culture conditions us to do. We're expected to hustle, hustle, hustle. You need to make time for your growth a non-negotiable way.

Practice Tips:

- Notice when you value yourself and your worth by what you do or do not achieve.
- Plan regular growth activities in your week.
- Experiment with different activities to discover what provides you

with the greatest experience of growth and freedom.

- Combine your growth activities with actions in other Key Areas of Life.

Habit #33: Practice a routine of daily and weekly growth activities that you consider non-negotiable.

Contribution

'The best way to find yourself is to lose yourself in the service of others.'
~ Mahatma Gandhi, leader of the Indian independence movement in British-ruled India

The Entrepreneur's 12 Key Areas of Life
Definition of the Area *Contribution*

Contribution: *The extent to which you are helping to achieve or causing to bring about things in the world that matter and are important to you.*

For as far back as we can look, man has looked for the meaning of life. The search for life's meaning has produced much philosophical, scientific, theological, and metaphysical speculation throughout history. What is our purpose here?

When people get connected to what that purpose is for *them*, it gives them a lot of power. If you ask the most famous and successful people in the world about their purposes you will get down to a common seed. That seed is about making a difference. One of our *Amorvita* Associates, Shawn, has listened to thousands of hours of interviews of famous and successful people. Every single one of them wants to make a difference in the world. They all use a variety of different avenues to do so but that is the common commitment.

Why is experiencing contribution as a working area in life important for achieving freedom? If contributing is not a key part of how you live your life, you're going to find that something's missing. You may have a successful business but will likely still feel unfulfilled. You just have to peel away the layers to find that everybody wants to contribute.

You can find great evidence for this by looking at our young children. They want to help all the time. They're always asking, 'Can I help you do that Mommy?' or saying, 'I can do that Daddy,' or 'Can I help you?' By the time they're at the age where they go to school we've ruined it with, 'No, just go watch TV or play your video games.' But that desire to contribute is always there, underneath. Everyone has it.

People are on the planet to contribute. Shawn's family has two charities that they work with. It's not uncommon to find entrepreneurs connected with non-profits. Her family raises funds for teens with diabetes. Her husband is diabetic and his father and grandmother both died from diabetes complications. They are also long-time supporters of the *Children With Aids Foundation*. Her uncle died of aids in 1993 and her sister was the foundation spokesperson for many years. Involvement in this work gives the people in Shawn's family meaning in their lives and purpose.

Find something that you're passionate about that you can get behind and support. If you don't, you may wake up one day thinking, *What the heck did I do with my life?* You might make lots of money but you have to leave it all behind. When you are about to die and remember that you can't take any of it with you, will you wish you made more of a difference?

As I mentioned earlier, when we get jammed in our businesses, the first area of our lives to get sacrificed is usually well-being. The second tends to be social relationships – we'll stop spending time with friends and family. The third area we tend to neglect is our contribution.

A big regret of people confronting death was not making the difference they wanted. No one says, 'I wish I was dying with more money in the bank.' Or, 'I wish I had had a bigger house.' Almost everyone says, 'I wish I'd had the courage to live a life true to myself,' according to Bonnie Ware in *The Top Five Regrets of the Dying*.[13]

Making a difference for the people you care about is a contribution. When your loved ones feel loved, respected and their dreams are fulfilled – that's contribution. Contribution does not have to be about a charity or helping the homeless. It can be about making a difference with your children. Having them lit up because you made it to all their soccer games could be the contribution of your life. They might never get over that.

Contributing isn't always about making a difference with something outside

[13] bronnieware.com/regrets-of-the-dying

of your circle. It's about making a difference with someone or something that matters to you. It could even be with your cherished pet. The important thing is simply that you're making a difference with something or someone outside of you.

A *Time* article on longevity said that 'helping others helps you live longer.'[14] The benefits of contribution can include:

- reduced early mortality rates by 22%
- reduced rates of depression
- increased sense of life satisfaction and well-being
- increased social contact
- reduced loneliness
- lower dementia risk

People get off track thinking it has to look a certain way. They want it to be big, or nothing. Contribution could be as easy as complimenting your 90-year-old neighbour on her roses. That's contribution because it's making a difference for others and/or the world rather than for yourself.

Start thinking about your contribution. It will set you free in your business and in your life!

Practice Tips:

- Get in the practice of looking outside of yourself and into the world for ways to contribute.
- Ask yourself the question, what kind of difference would it make for you if you contributed today?
- Discover something that matters to you and start taking actions in that area.
- Be intentional every morning about how you are going to make a difference either inside or outside of your circle.
- Allow others the joy of contributing to you without opposition or argument. Don't rob them of the gift of giving to another.

Habit #34: Every morning ask yourself, who will you contribute to today and how will you contribute to life?

---

[14] healthland.time.com/2013/08/23/helping-others-helps-you-to-live-longer

Business

'Nothing is really work unless you would rather be doing something else.'
~ James M. Barrie novelist and playwright, *Peter Pan*

The Entrepreneur's 12 Key Areas of Life
Definition of the Area *Business*

Business: *The activities you are engaged in that include your regular occupation, profession, trade or devotion of time and attention to acquiring knowledge on an academic subject.*

As we discussed in Habit #17, *Know your Why*, for an entrepreneur, the experience of freedom is tied to fulfilling a higher purpose. Either you run a business that fulfills your vision, mission and passion in the world, or, you have a business that provides access to fulfilling on what you're passionate about. If your business isn't built on one of these two foundations, you're setting yourself up for failure.

In the absence of your higher purpose, survival-driven thoughts, feelings and behaviours fill the space. You'll find yourself running your business with the experience of doing it because you have to. There will be little joy or satisfaction and definitely no freedom present.

I have always followed a higher calling or passion in my own businesses. That was not always the case in my days of working in the corporate world. While most of my early career in the telecommunications sector was fulfilling, that was not always the case.

At one point, I accepted a role with an international advertising agency. My severance package was running out when a recruiter approached me with an opportunity. I was clear that the job would not fulfill my higher calling, but I took it anyway. I was in survival mode from the start. I expected to find relationships like the ones I had had in my previous agency. This was not the case. Every day the situation became harder to accept and to survive. And it didn't provide access to what I loved either.

Can you work in a business that you don't love, not feel trapped and experience freedom? Of course you can – that is, if it provides *access* to fulfilling on what you *do* love. It doesn't matter if you climb through piles of garbage every day for work. If that business provides a pathway to fulfill on your higher purpose, it gives you an access to freedom.

Maybe it gives you time freedom to travel to Africa to build schools every year. Or perhaps you have a passion for the environment and it provides access to sitting on a board of directors and being able to influence key decisions. What's important is that you must be clear how your business connects to your higher purpose. Don't do anything just to survive. That is a low form of existence.

The first question entrepreneurs ask themselves when they discover that they're surviving is: *What do I do now?* When you're surviving your business you feel trapped. It occurs like your options are limited. But, you put all this time into growing your business…it doesn't make any sense to just give it up and walk away. It's a catch 22 situation.

I have a good friend of mine going through this right now. She has a successful social media business. It no longer excites her or fulfills her passion. But it's a profitable, established business that takes care of her financial needs. Quitting the business is just not an option for her right now. So she's going to continue to run the business on the side while she pursues things that she *is* passionate about.

What about those of us who love what we do but it doesn't fulfill on our higher purpose? Perhaps you started the business out of a hobby you enjoy. There is no question you feel fulfilled and satisfied. But isn't that the point – to create a successful business doing something you love? In my experience that feeling of satisfaction has a limited lifespan. Eventually, you'll feel like something is missing. You'll start trying new things to fill the gap and nothing seems to work. Connecting to a higher purpose, however, and taking actions consistent with it, returns an experience of freedom.

When you find yourself in a world of survival, ensure you do what you need to do in order to be able to operate from one of the two options: Either that your business is aligned with your higher purpose and you fulfill that purpose *directly* through it, or it indirectly provides a *pathway* to fulfilling it. If neither of these is the case, you have some simple options that can make a difference. You do not need to drastically change your business or quit.

One option is to create a *new* business that *does* fulfill on your higher purpose. You'll need to change the way you manage the first business. Run it in a way that it frees up hours in your week to work in the new business. We've already looked at habits to support doing this in previous chapters. Focus on automation and delegation to free up time.

Another option is to focus on having your business be more *profitable* as well as efficient—profitable enough to provide financial resources to make a difference with your higher purpose, and efficient to free up some of your time so you can start to work on what you're passionate about.

Take on living from the approach that you are unwilling to just survive. Your courageous step into the entrepreneurial world was and is all about creating freedom. Make up your mind that you will not accept anything less. You deserve it. Are you willing to do what you need to do to earn that freedom?

Practice Tips:

- Be clear about your higher purpose by completing the necessary work to uncover it (refer to Habit# 14 for how to do this).
- Make sure that your business is fulfilling your higher purpose either directly or indirectly.
- When your higher purpose is not being fulfilled, create a pathway to provide access to it.
- Work with a business coach who supports creating actions aligned with your higher purpose.
- Don't tolerate surviving your business. It's the foundational access to your freedom.

Habit #35: Identify where you are surviving your business and take immediate actions to create freedom.

Wewalth

'What's money? A man is a success if he gets up in the morning and goes to bed at night and in between does what he wants to do.'
~ Bob Dylan, singer-songwriter

The Entrepreneur's 12 Key Areas of Life
Definition of the Area *Wealth*

Wealth: *The actions and activities you take to manage and create money and things that are worth money including property, assets, stocks, funds and resources.*

I know of no other Key Area that seems to impact an entrepreneur's experience of freedom more than the area of *Wealth*. When there is plenty of wealth, freedom is present, and when there isn't plenty of wealth, it's not. So many business owners define their success by money. When there are financial challenges, as there inevitably are from time to time, they take it personally. During these times think they're failures or tell themselves something equally damaging to their self-image.

That's not to say that wealth is not an important Key Area of Life. In many ways, a strong foundation of wealth provides flexibility and options. It provides the ability to hire a team, pay for social and recreation activities, provide for a family and much more.

I once had to take 4 months off from working on *Amorvita* to deal with my health. That put a tremendous financial strain on both me and the business. There is only so much you can do to reduce expenses. Fixed costs do not care if you are earning an income of not.

The situation meant extending payment terms on our payables and maxing out credit lines. There was a short period of time when I considered closing our doors. It seemed like the simpler option and I felt trapped by the accumulating debt. There was definitely no freedom present.

At the time, I was clear I was a failure. I was angry with my body for being weak and not giving me what I needed. I was embarrassed and ashamed to tell people what was going on or to ask for support. My higher purpose was going to need to get fulfilled by someone else. It was as clear as day that I was not up to the task. I learned the hard way that I needed to create a plan in order to turn my situation around – a plan for both my situation at the time *and* my future. I did, and I turned the situation around. But it all started with creating a financial plan for myself and the business.

There are two major issues related to wealth that I encounter when working with clients. One is that they often say they're not earning the kind of money they started their businesses to make. The second is that they haven't created a secure financial future for themselves.

The importance of dealing with wealth in the present is minor compared to thinking about the future. What plans do you have for when you stop working? What do you have in place if you were to get ill or have an accident that prevented you from working? What kind of financial legacy do you want to leave for your family? These are the big, important questions that go beyond the worries of today's cash flow.

So many entrepreneurs are short sighted in this Key Area. They focus only on last month's bills getting paid, or where the money is coming from for their next big training investment. Although these are important considerations as well, there's too little attention on long-term cash flow planning, retirement, contingency planning and legacy.

Clients often say they have no space in their minds or schedules to even think about anything beyond the next few weeks. That's how little freedom entrepreneurs have in this area. I can't say that I was any different when I was contemplating the dire future of my business not that long ago.

I learned that even when you're in a crunch, you have to make the time to create the type of plan that will provide you freedom in both the short *and* long term. Freedom in this Key Area of Life will not just happen no matter how much you wish for it to or ignore it. This is no different than expecting to get healthier without exercising or eating better.

When creating a powerful relationship with wealth you must consider your hierarchy of needs. The first level to handle is the level of your basic needs: You need to eat, have a roof over your head, pay for heat, etc. Your business needs to be able to pay for this. If it cannot at least provide this, it may not be a business worth continuing.

The second level to consider is the business' basic needs. What does your business cost to operate on a monthly basis? This could include leasing costs, telecomm, electricity, software subscriptions, etc. Business owners often start layering in more than the basics at this level. All we're talking about is the bare bone essentials to have your business operate. A business must produce revenue at least equal to the business needs and your personal basic needs. In other words, the business needs to pay for itself and pay your salary so that you can pay for your basic needs.

Once you have those two basics covered you can start to add the successive levels in order. These include debt repayment, fun, emergency funds, retirement, legacy and living your ideal lifestyle. Adding and funding each level requires additional monthly income.

You want to create a plan that identifies a clear pathway from providing for your basic needs to enabling you to live your ideal lifestyle. Having this plan in place provides a strong sense of freedom. I completed my plan with all of the necessary milestones in the middle of my 4-month health crisis. Once I created the plan, I experienced an immediate release of pressure and stress. Solutions started coming to me immediately that were not there just moments before. My entire situation transformed. I felt better. I had freedom.

What's important to note is that the *circumstances* in my situation did not change. All that happened was there was a shift in my perspective; all from creating a clear pathway to each of my financial milestones for each successive level.

Practice Tips:

- Notice how much you define your self-image by your wealth. Remember that you are not your financial situation.
- Remember that the business' first priority is to provide you with the ability to pay for your basic needs.
- Take actions to ensure that the business is generating enough income to pay its basic needs and yours.
- Create a wealth plan with financial milestones from basic to living your ideal lifestyle.
- Set promise dates for each financial milestone and build your life plan to match.

Habit #36: Identify everything that lacks integrity in the area of *Wealth* and begin resolving each.

FEATURE INTERVIEW

Ken Honda is the #1 motivational speaker and best-selling author of self-development books in Japan (kenhonda.tokyo). He is a prolific and successful writer, selling more than 7 million copies of his texts since 2001. His writings bridge the topics of finance and self-help, focusing on creating and generating personal wealth and happiness through deeper self-honesty. Ken counts an audience of about 1 in every 20 people across the country who listen to his podcasts and recorded lectures and attend his seminars.

He has been an entrepreneur his entire professional life and never worked for anyone else. He started his first business at the age of 23 and was financially independent by 29 years old when he semi-retired and spent the next four years raising his daughter. His financial expertise comes from owning and managing several businesses, including an accounting company, a management consulting firm and a venture capital corporation.

What does entrepreneurial freedom mean to you personally?

People who want to be entrepreneurs want to experience freedom in every area of life. Now that includes financial freedom, freedom of time, emotional freedom and maybe even social freedom. Freedom is really every area of your life. So if you become successful as an entrepreneur you can gain all the freedom that you want, but what's tricky is that in the process of becoming a successful entrepreneur, you might have to give up certain freedoms. For example time-wise, you would be so busy for a while you would give up freedom of time. In the process of making it, you will probably lose some financial freedom too. Also, you may feel so stressful that you might lose emotional freedom. It's a tough road too. I think one of the freedoms is you want to say whatever you want and you want to do whatever you want, as long as it is legal and serves people. You don't have to care how you look. I have long hair which is very unique for Japanese men.

What three habits contribute the most to you achieving that freedom?

The first habit is a strong desire to do everything necessary to achieve your goals. A lot of people give up part way through. You have to be willing to commit yourself and follow through 100%.

The second habit is being creative. You face mistakes, setbacks and obstacles along every step of the way. You have to prepare a resource of ideas and creative strategies to come back from all the failure that you are most likely to face in the process.

Number three is getting the right help from other people. Entrepreneurs are often too independent to ask other people for help. When the chance comes along, don't automatically assume that they will not help you out. Most people enjoy helping others. I'm sure as an entrepreneur you must like helping people, so you must give people a chance to help you.

If you develop those 3 habits you are almost guaranteed to make it.

Give us a picture window into how you start your days.

The first thing I do in the morning is to put myself into a state of gratitude in the present moment. I'm a very goal oriented person so I like to prepare for each day by going over my schedule and visualizing all the fun and abundance that's in store for that day. No two days are alike for me. I enjoy a lot of freedom in my schedule. I enjoy talking to thousands of people at seminars, travelling around Japan, meeting interesting people and interviews such as this. I feel so thankful for opportunities that I see each day. The morning is an important time to put myself in the right state of mind to face that day.

I wrote in my work that it is about raising up your sincerity of heart. That means raising your vibration. By thanking people, people tend to thank you back. If you are full of gratitude, people automatically feel the gratitude coming from you. They give you more positive feedback and they will be nicer to you.

What's the most important habit entrepreneurs should have?

The most important thing is to stay curious about your life. Because you never know what is going to happen. If you stay curious about your future, I think your success is guaranteed. A lot of people lose curiosity about the future possibilities or potential markets. As long as you follow your curiosity, you'll never lose the passion to change your life and the lives of other people.

Any final thoughts to share about entrepreneurial freedom?

Entrepreneurship is a very interesting way of life. In order to gain all the freedom you desire, you have to give up certain freedoms in the process and that's the tricky part. You have to decide how long it's going to take for you to succeed. Shorter is better, but if you want to try and make it too quickly, you will lose everything. You have to be realistic about how much time it's going to take and just go for it. A lot of people don't plan things out and just go for it anyways, losing everything on the way. So please be creative and follow the passion and curiosity in your heart. You will find everything that you wish for in life. Wishing everybody lots of luck.

CHAPTER **FIVE**

STRUCTURE

Visualize And Create Your Day

'I believe that visualization is one of the most powerful means of achieving personal goals.'
~ Harvey Mackay, businessman, author of seven *New York Times* bestselling
books and syndicated columnist in over 100 newspapers

There are tremendous benefits in doing the work to plan tomorrow before your head hits the pillow today. Neuroscientists at Harvard have demonstrated that your brain doesn't know the difference between something that's real or something that's imagined. Understanding this provides a great access to support you in having freedom.

Inc.com stated that one of the most important business skills every entrepreneur must have is planning.[15] Most people don't spend enough of their time planning. If you are not the CEO you're likely going to spend more time in execution than planning. But in your own business, and in your life, if you say you want to do something and don't have a plan for it, you're fooling yourself. Without a plan, at best what you'll accomplish is a fluke. We already touched on the importance of planning in earlier habits.

If you go to sleep without taking care of tomorrow's schedule, you have a limited chance of it actually happening. The world is going to throw you curve balls. Life is full of unforeseen things coming your way. The only

---

[15] http://www.inc.com/murray-newlands/5-most-important-business-skills-every-entrepreneur-must-have.html

decent chance you have at accomplishing what you set out to accomplish is to have your schedule work for you rather than you working for it.

You have an opportunity to take advantage of the amazing phenomenon of your brain. Remember, it cannot tell the difference between the real and imagined. The imagined in the form of visualization can be a powerful tool. Olympic athletes use visualization to create neural pathways that enable them to improve performance.

Russian scientists who conducted a study comparing the training schedules of four groups of Olympic athletes.[16] Each group used a different combination of physical and mental training:

- Group one: 100% physical training
- Group two: 75% physical training, 25% mental training
- Group three: 50% physical training, 50% mental training
- Group four: 25% physical training, 75% mental training

The scientists found that the fourth group—that had undergone the highest percentage of mental training—performed the best during the Olympics. Planning and visualizing your day the night before has your subconscious mind work to support you.

I tell my private clients not to go to bed until they have looked at their schedule for the next day. I want them to ensure nothing is about to come and bite them in the butt. This way they head into their day prepared.

You might ask, how is someone supposed to know that something is going to come bite them in the butt? Surely they are not a fortune teller. This may be true; but, there are things one can do to anticipate problems and adjust in advance to avoid them. When I look at tomorrow in my calendar, I'm asking myself the question, *Did anything happened today that could get in the way of what I am doing tomorrow? Is there any follow-up I have to add in tomorrow?* For example, maybe a client called that day and they have a big issue that I need to manage with them the next day. I might have to move things around to make space to ensure I can do it.

Because I look at my calendar the night before, I can get in communication with whomever I need to in advance. If I need to, I can ask them to move our meeting or call. It gives me the benefit of giving them advance notice versus calling them just before our appointment. People appreciate the

---

[16] businessinsider.com/olympic-athletes-and-power-of-visualization-2015-1

advanced warning so they can make adjustments to their day as well.

Advanced planning work is important so you can ensure that what is in your calendar gets taken care of. It enables you to have integrity with what you said to yourself that you would do. Planning is for *you*. It enables you to have *power* in relationship to your calendar, so you can avoid feeling like a victim to your schedule.

Planning is also important for your relationships. One thing people often don't realize is that there is an impact on the people around you when your life is not planned. Sometimes entrepreneurs think they should not have to plan time for themselves and others. They feel that they have the flexibility to play it by ear and work it out as they go. That's what they think freedom is. But if you're working 80 hours a week and don't plan to have time to see your partner or children, that will be problematic.

My favourite excuse for entrepreneurs not taking the time to plan is that they don't have time. The time you save by not planning is *more* than offset by the time wasted due to a lack of planning.

I also love the I'm-not-a-planner-I-like-to-go-with-the-flow-and-it-works-for-me reason. I would have loved to see us launch any space mission that way. We're just going to go with the flow and get the lander to Mars. That sounds totally ridiculous right? Don't you think you sound just as ridiculous running your business, life and tomorrow without a plan?

The second last thing in my calendar before bed is: *My day is complete and I am more than ready for tomorrow.* When I'm done, my mind is clear and I can go read for fun. There's nothing left for me to worry about. The more you can do at night to have things be setup for the next day, the better. I sleep like a baby when my plan is done.

I was leading a workshop recently and one of the women said that she creates her day first thing in the morning. While I don't believe there's necessarily a 'right' way or 'wrong' way to do this, I always recommend my clients do it before they go to bed versus when they first wake up. Then you don't have to take all that unfinished stuff in your mind to bed with you. You wake up with a clear mind, ready and knowing what you are about to step into. Otherwise you're starting out the day wondering, *What crap do I need to work out today?* It's absolutely worth it to take the time to create your day the night before!

Lastly, rather than thinking you need to come up with something new in order to manage your time, take a look at what's already out there. Why reinvent the wheel when there are plenty of successful people you can copy? Find a scheduling system that works for you and start to take on visualizing and creating your day.

Practice Tips:

- Plan your calendar at least two weeks out to anticipate the demands on your time.
- Plan to do something for pleasure after creating your next day and before going to sleep.
- Take time in advance to visualize your day and how it's going to go.
- When setting up your day always be thinking from a place of, *What could possibly bite me in the butt tomorrow?*
- Value other people's time. Communicate changes of plans to your family and colleagues as soon as you can see that something needs to be moved.

Habit #37: Set-up, create and visualize your day before you go to sleep the night before.

Schedule Quarterly and Weekly Promises

'If you don't design your own life plan, chances are you'll fall into someone else's plan. And guess what they have planned for you? Not much.'
~ Jim Rohn, entrepreneur, author and motivational speaker

In earlier chapters we looked at the importance of creating your 10-year vision. From there we created waypoints or milestones to reach at 5 years, 3 years and 1 year. This habit lights the path from today to your 10-year vision. It involves the creation of quarterly and weekly *promises.*

People often say that they have quarterly 'goals' instead of promises. The dictionary defines a goal as, 'something that you are trying to do or achieve.'[17] A promise, however, is defined as, 'a statement telling someone that you will definitely do something or that something will definitely happen in the

---

[17] merriam-webster.com/dictionary/goal

future.'[18] Setting goals sets you up for the wishy-washy possibility that they might or might not happen. Making promises sets you up for powerfully bringing your visions to fruition.

A revenue 'goal' would sound something like: 'I aim to achieve $60,000 in revenue in the next quarter.' Restated as a promise it would sound something like: 'I promise that I will achieve $60,000 or more in revenue before the end of the next quarter.'

I am not interested in what you are going to *try* to achieve in the next quarter. I am *highly* interested in what you declare will definitely happen.

People, including entrepreneurs, relate differently to making a promise versus setting a goal. From now until 13 weeks from now (the next quarter) you are only making promises about what you will achieve. Don't think of them as 'goals' anymore. Of course, you still need your plan. But all you need is your plan and your promises. A goal is a *desired* result, whereas a plan and a set of promises gives you *access to achieving* results.

If you resist planning or have never done any, start with a quarterly plan. You can always work your way up to longer time periods. Quarterly creations actually begin with an ending or the completion of something. The start of creating a new year begins with the completion of the previous year. There are lots of different resources online for how to do this. Simply do a search on 'complete my year.' Most business and personal coaches outline some version of this process.

The ideal time to complete your year is sometime between Christmas and the beginning of the New Year. Don't start a new year with any 'should ofs,' 'could ofs,' or 'didn't dos.' Follow the process you choose to use in entirety so you can to have the entire year be complete and a done deal.

Follow the same process for each quarter. It's important to do this completion work before creating your promises for the next quarter. About a week before the end of each quarter, answer this series of questions:

- What did you accomplish?
- What worked?
- What didn't work?
- What actions did you take that you were proud of?
- What was missing?

---

[18] merriam-webster.com/dictionary/promise

- What could you have done that you didn't do?

You created your big picture quarterly items when you completed your 1-year plan (refer to Habit #21). When you know what you want to do by the end of the year, you're able to create your third quarter promises. Once those are complete, you'll know where you need to end up by the end of the second quarter. You can then create those promises. The same is true for the first quarter. Once you're clear about the next quarter you can make weekly *promises*.

As you get to the end of each quarter, you'll find that things have changed since the beginning of the year. New opportunities may have come along. You may have made strategic choices not to do something you had planned at the beginning of the year. Revisions may be required to adjust your course.

The quarterly planning habit is great because you can revise your path and promises throughout the year as you need to. That's much better than blaming yourself for what you didn't do. It takes away the morality conversations that negatively affect your self-image. All you deal with is reality.

The reality is that you will accomplish what you promise. Everything else is an accident. You just need to course correct around accidents as you go, and get back on track.

When you plan for something and make promises toward it, there is an 80% better chance of you actually accomplishing it than if you hadn't. Pareto's 80:20 rule applies to a lot of things. I was laughing with my colleague the other day about people who question why it's 80:20 and not 90:10. If that is where you have your attention you are missing the entire point of the conversation! It doesn't matter if you think of it as 80:20 or 90:10 – what matters is simply that the 10 or 20% of time and focus that you spend on planning returns 80% or 90% of your results. Planning and making promises are *that* important.

Planning includes planning and promises for all 12 Key Areas of Life. My plan for my *Well-being* includes completing an Ironman event in 2018. That plan started four and half years before the anticipated date of the race. *Amorvita's* team events are planned over a year in advance. That's what works in order for people to be able to make decisions about things in their lives in enough advance and to be able to be at those events.

I watch entrepreneurs try all sorts of different ways of running their lives. Some ways work and some don't. Why not follow a path that works and produces results? Planning in the way I've outlined throughout this book, works.

When people *don't* plan there are some common consequences our team has observed:

- A higher frequency and intensity of issues in their business and in the rest of their life.
- Major unexpected issues come up every couple of days.
- The issues appear to be unexpected but could have been anticipated with planning.
- They are more tired than other people.
- They're always trying to pull something out of thin air.
- Higher incidence of chronic fatigue or burnout.
- They experience plenty of stress and stress kills.

A research team led by Carnegie Mellon University's Sheldon Cohen has found that chronic psychological stress is associated with the body losing its ability to regulate the inflammatory response.[19] The research shows for the first time that the effects of psychological stress on the body's ability to regulate inflammation can promote the development and progression of disease.

When you create a plan and promises to keep you on track, you set yourself up for success and grant yourself freedom.

Practice Tips:

- Complete your year between Christmas and the New Year before creating your plan for the upcoming year. Get coaching support as needed.
- Make *promises* rather than setting 'goals' for your quarterly and weekly plans.
- Create your quarterly promises from your 1-year plan.
- Remember that things change. Your quarterly and weekly promises will need to be adjusted as you progress though the year. Don't take the fact that you have to make changes personally.
- Include all 12 Key Areas of Life in your quarterly and weekly planning.

---

[19] sciencedaily.com/releases/2012/04/120402162546.htm

Habit #38: Schedule time during in the last week of each quarter to create quarterly and weekly promises.

Set Boundaries

'No' is a complete sentence.'
~ Anne Lamott, political activist, public speaker and writing teacher

Many entrepreneurs don't draw lines between the 12 Key Areas of Life. This is especially true between *Business* and the other 11 areas. Sometimes they work until 2 AM and won't get enough rest. There's often no shortage of work because there is always the next thing to do. If I wanted to, I could deprive myself of sleep and work on all types of different ideas and never stop.

If there's an endless supply of work, some action is needed in order to experience freedom. You must be able to set boundaries or draw lines in your life over which work is not allowed to cross. I call one of these boundaries your 'cut-off time.'

A 'cut-off time' is a time that you declare you will not work later than. My current cut-off time is 6:30 PM. Working after this time is an exception and a deliberate choice. Time after 6:30 PM is reserved for other things in my life.

A study published in 2014 by John Pencavel of Stanford University quantified the relationship between hours worked and productivity. Research shows that output falls sharply after a 50-hour work week, and falls off a cliff after 55 hours.[20] What's shocking is that someone who puts in 70 hours produces nothing more with those extra 15 hours. You think you're making a difference in your business by grinding it out, but you're not.

My endurance coach, Nat, has an incredibly powerful relationship to freedom as an entrepreneur. But it didn't start out that way! I don't know why I was so surprised to find this out. Maybe it was because he's a great example of a business owner operating with peace and freedom. His first year was such a slow start that he didn't get overwhelmed. But by the time

---

[20] cnbc.com/2015/01/26/working-more-than-50-hours-makes-you-less-productive.html

he got to year two it got out of control.

Nat embraced the stay up until 2 AM, get little sleep, grind it out mentality. He stopped operating that way by accident when he started training for the Ironman. He started spending all sorts of time working out and nurturing himself.

He began to notice himself feeling much better and happier. He fell asleep when he went to bed and not during the middle of the day, in meetings or at workshops with other people. He enjoyed being active and began to take steps to operate like that all the time.

I asked Nat what he learned from that experience. He shared that for him boundaries are one of those fine line things that you can't be 100% militant about. Whatever boundaries you draw are a guideline to consider in managing all the Key Areas of Life. But it's super important to have that guideline. He became clear about the need to recognize his business as a separate entity from himself. He discovered that if he allows the business to take more than it gives back, it's unsustainable.

You may choose to make a calculated decision to engage in a detrimental situation for a short time. For example, I am going go with only 4 hours of sleep for the next two days to complete this project. However, if you choose this path, watch yourself to ensure it remains an exception. And, to enter a detrimental situation thinking, *I have to give everything I can and hope it works out* does not work. It's tough not having an end date for how long the *Business* area is going to take a priority over other Key Areas of life. You could wake up one day and it's 5 years later and you are totally drained and in poor health. You won't be capable of taking care of business then or in the future.

You can draw boundaries while also leaving room to make exceptions. You may feel compelled to do an extra hour one day or do one week of longer days. When the exception ends, go back to the original way of operating right away.

Some people think setting boundaries is the opposite of having freedom. But the boundaries are not constraints or a jail that you're in. On the contrary, boundaries give you freedom to say, 'I have boundaries and I choose them because I know what they create and enable.' And you can also say, 'I have freedom to *not* choose my boundaries if that's what I need to do' when you need to do that.

Make sure it doesn't become, 'I have the freedom to work until 10 PM every night because that's my 'choice." Then three months later, 10 o'clock at night has become the new norm and it's no longer freedom. All of a sudden you feel constrained that you are working 14 hours a day and the freedom you had before is gone.

It's important to remember that we're all human and we have some finite capacities. Start examining the areas of your life where setting boundaries would make a difference for you. We'll examine how this conversation relates to the area of *Being Well Rested* in Habit #49.

Consider also where you need to set emotional boundaries. There are times when we contribute to people and are in a supportive role. There's a line for most people where the balance of giving versus receiving needs to change. That's the time to set a boundary and start saying 'no.' Sometimes the boundary gets pushed so far that you end up saying to yourself, I can't take anymore! Recognize that at that point you need to be emotionally supported.

Setting boundaries involves maintaining and setting limits on many different fronts. For this habit we focused mostly on the boundary of a cut-off time. Start here and notice the difference implementing this habit makes. Then get creative and see where other boundaries could make a difference.

Practice Tips:

- Have a cut-off time that you don't work beyond after.
- Have exceptions be exceptions and not your new norm.
- Share your cut-off time with your team and clients and be proud of it.
- Establish healthy boundaries in other areas of your life like sleep and emotional exchanges.

  Habit #39: Establish a daily cut-off time and honour it.

Take Days Off

'Each person deserves a day away in which no problems are confronted [and] no solutions searched for. Each of us needs to withdraw from the cares which will not withdraw from us.'
~ Maya Angelou, poet, memoirist and civil rights activist

Sometimes non-entrepreneurs get unsettled by how busy an entrepreneur's schedule is. We could have a perfectly harmonious schedule of the 12 Key Areas and that would still occur as a crazy world to some. But no matter how busy our schedules get, it's important to take days off.

It's funny how many times people say to me that they want to be considerate of my busy schedule. It's not that I don't appreciate the thoughtful sentiments. Quite the opposite; I love considerate and caring people in my life. But the truth is, I have far more freedom and flexibility in my schedule than someone working a corporate 9 to 5 j-o-b. And I don't often hear the same considerations extended to them.

One challenge I see with clients taking time off is that often their office workspace is inside their home. They find it challenging to get away from their work when it's just across the hall or in the next room. It's so easy to access and can be hard to stay away from. And what's worse, I sometimes see entrepreneurs struggling with the feeling that they haven't done enough during their work hours.

When we're doing what we love and are passionate about it doesn't feel like work. There is an immense amount of joy to it. You want to do more and more of it and quickly it becomes seven days a week that you are working on your joyous passion.

But even still, your body and your brain actually need to take breaks. We have looked at this fact in many other habits. We're now clear that we are not performing at our best level when working on our businesses seven days a week. And yet this is the area of an entrepreneur's life around which I get the most resistance from clients.

Other business coaches share that they get the most pushback from clients in this particular area as well. I have a colleague in Vancouver who asks clients to go out for a date night with their spouse and people push back.

Time off to attend to other important things in life is important. In this particular discussion, I'm speaking specifically about taking *days off* – full days off where you do no work whatsoever. When I say no work, I literally mean *no work*: No checking emails, no responding to texts, no clearing voicemail…none of it. If your cell phone is your work phone, you might get a personal message and check your voice mail on your day off. But when you hear a work-related message, hit the save button and deal with it when you are actually back to work.

I say to take at least one full day off per week. The ideal that I coach my clients to achieve is two per week. When I say this at speaking events I usually get some variation of, 'Oh my God! I can't even imagine doing that!'

But you know at some level that this makes sense. The instant, almost guaranteed first reaction, is to respond with why it's not possible for you, and to tell me why it won't work in your business. Yet you don't like that your automatic reaction is disbelief. That leaves you to confront just how much freedom is absent from your life.

Often the mind goes to, *I'm an entrepreneur and entrepreneurs don't get days off. Maybe we get moments off, or a couple of hours perhaps, but a whole day?!* Let's be clear: I am not saying a day; I am saying *two days* per week. I shared this once with a client and she said, 'That's like a vacation in the entrepreneurial world. Two days is a vacation.'

Something I started with my stubborn clients is to have them schedule four 12-hour periods per week of no work. Some people cannot wrap their minds around taking an entire 24-hour period off in one week. Somehow 12-hour blocks makes it easier to swallow. They can always put two 12-hour blocks together later when they get more comfortable with the idea of taking time off.

I was chatting with Cynthia, my photographer about this. She had the typical reaction when I talked about taking 2 days off. She said to me, 'I don't need a day off because this doesn't feel like work. The more it doesn't feel like work, the more I will respond to social invitations with a 'no.''

I asked her to play devil's advocate with her upcoming Saturday shoot schedule and she agreed. I said, 'Imagine if you had Friday off to do whatever you wanted. You could go for a walk, go on a date, read a book, get a mani-pedi or go to a movie in the middle of the afternoon. Imagine if for the entire day on Friday you didn't do any work at all.'

Then I asked, 'How do you think your shoot on Saturday would go if you had a day off versus working on Friday?' She got excited at the idea. She said she would be more relaxed, more at ease and more creative. She'd be more open to trying new things in her photos. She would feel less like she was coming out of a grind.

In this situation, what is true for Cynthia is true for every entrepreneur: When you give yourself time to relax it increases your productivity and creativity. You're more effective going back to your business after giving yourself a full day off.

When you say to yourself, *I'm not really working today*, then do emails and other work, you don't actually take time off. You don't grant yourself any freedom when you do this. Instead, you set yourself up for a negative set of feelings about yourself and your ability to manage your time. Set and take your days off. Your business, and the rest of your life, will thank you for it.

Practice Tips:

- When you're taking time off be completely off work – no emails, texts or calls related to your business.
- Start your time off habit by taking 12-hour blocks of time off first.
- If you are currently taking no fun days off, start with one day per week and work from there.
- Train your team and clients to know that when you are off you are not available.
- Create structures to deal with any emergencies that may arise in your business while you're on a day off.

Habit #40: Take two full days off per week and at least one full week off per quarter.

Plan Creative Days

'Happiness is not in the mere possession of money; it lies in the joy of achievement [and] in the thrill of creative effort.'
~ Franklin D. Roosevelt, President of the United States

Let's assume we have now managed to get you to take one or two days off a week. The next thing to look at is taking one day out of what's remaining in your schedule for a creative day.

A creative day is for you to work *ON* your business and not *IN* your business. Creative days are not interrupted by other things. You don't schedule any phone calls or meetings. You manage email, texts and voicemail at the beginning and end of the day. During the day, you turn all of those distractions off.

I love my creative days. They usually involve me relocating to an inspirational location to work. In the summertime, I like to be in the park, by the pool or down by the water. I take my laptop and work on my plans and creative projects like building programs.

Being in a creative environment gives me access to new ideas that might not flow so easily at my desk. It's a day I get to spend with myself and build the business. From time to time, I will invite others to join me in my creative environment.

When I talk with entrepreneurs about this, the first thing I am usually asked is, 'What am I going to spend an entire day working on every week?'

We can start with some of the items outlined in previous habits. It's a perfect time to:

- Create your 5-year, 3-year and 1-year plans
- Develop your quarterly and weekly promises
- Educate yourself on your business or industry
- Create newsletters
- Plan tasks to delegate
- Develop workflow processes
- Create new programs
- Develop new content

Why not just do these things during the rest of the week? Why set aside one entire day for these tasks? The answer is *momentum*. By moving creative tasks to one day, it leaves 4 or 5 days in your week free to work concentratedly IN your business. Have you ever noticed it takes you time to get into the flow and rhythm of making sales calls?

It also costs you time to have to keep switching gears between different kinds of work during your day. My endurance coach has me do bricks as part of my Ironman preparation. A brick has you jump off a bike and then immediately start running. The goal is to improve how fast you can shake the wobbly feeling as you transition from one form of exertion to the another. The same is relevant in working on your business. Every time you stop to transition, it takes time for you to get back in the flow. When you keep your creative tasks to one day you get into a creative flow.

Outside of your days off and your creative day, the remaining days are for being in the flow of handling everything else to have your business be successful. Larger blocks of time are better than a lot of smaller chunks that add up to the same total because you aren't wasting time switching gears.

The biggest temptation is to turn creative days into your 'emergency' days. That's when you relate to creative days as the-place-everything-gets-done-that-is-an-emergency-this-week. Because surely that client issue is more important than creating your 5-year plan…and what's the difference if you do that plan this week or next, anyway? It takes rigor and discipline to protect this time in your calendar. When you do, you will never regret it.

Entrepreneurs often say they don't have time to plan. It continues to be the single biggest weakness for most business owners. Implementing this habit handles that for you. It creates regular time in your week to be imaginative and to build a strong, successful business.

Sometimes I'm asked by people who work in creative businesses if this habit applies to them too. Absolutely, it does. Just because you're in a creative field does not mean you automatically spend an appropriate amount of time planning. It can also be a day to be completely creative without calls or other distractions. Regardless of what field you're in, that could provide a world of difference.

I'm always amazed at how much I get accomplished during my creative days. Some days it seems like I'm the Marvel comics character *The Flash* and I'm moving and creating at super speed. Personally, I enjoy the momentum that focus and working somewhere that inspires me provides. I never seem to have as many creative pauses on these days.

When you schedule and take your creative days, you'll notice a significant increase in your creative output. Watch how many of those nagging projects get completed. Watch your experience of freedom increase as you cross things off that long list.

Practice Tips:

- Plan your creative days several weeks out. Block them off and prevent appointments from getting scheduled during them.
- Keep required administrative tasks restricted to the beginning and

end of your creative days.

- Relocate from your normal working environment for your creative days. Find a place that inspires you.
- Schedule your creative activities in larger blocks of time.
- It's better to take the entire day or schedule one or two 4-hour blocks rather than scheduling eight 1-hour blocks.
- Train your team, clients and vendors to know that you are not available on creative days.

Habit #41: Schedule a creative day each week and go somewhere inspiring.

Be Intentional About Messaging

'One look at an email can rob you of 15 minutes of focus. One call on your cell phone, one tweet [or] one instant message can destroy your schedule, forcing you to move meetings or blow off really important things, like love and friendship.'
~ Jacqueline Leo, magazine editor and media producer

Messaging includes text, emails and social media messages. Entrepreneurs have a vested interest in being available and communicating well at all times. In today's busy digital world there are many channels to communicate with people. We're often on autopilot when it comes to managing and responding to messages. For many, freedom in a world of constant communication begs for some way to make messaging more efficient.

People and companies get lost in the back and forth of useless, needless conversation. It's because so many are on autopilot that things get out of control. We're purposeful about a lot of things in our business. Why is autopilot is our default mode when it comes to dealing with messages?

Text messages are the most intrusive of the bunch. Social media and email interruptions are a close second. Most people find it difficult to leave a text message sitting there without responding. Your phone goes, *Ding*, you see it's a text message and what's the first thing you do? You reply, of course.

Not only does being at the beck and call of your phone interrupt your focus, it can also be very unprofessional. A personal pet peeve of mine is when people text in inappropriate places, like in the middle of a meeting.

They receive a text and say, 'One second, I just need to reply to this text,' or something similar. I am certain that you have me scheduled from 10-10:30 AM. If I check your calendar I am also 100% certain that I will not find, *10:05-10:07 Reply to text message.* How in any professional setting does someone consider doing that to be OK?

Being intentional about messaging is an area that can be challenging for entrepreneurs. They can resist setting boundaries around messaging a lot. I can assure you, though, you will experience much more freedom in your business when you alter this for yourself.

To implement messaging boundaries, there are a couple of things to keep in mind. First, only check your email, texts and social media a fixed number of times a day. For me, that number is twice per day. This is a practice where one rule does not apply to everyone. Every business is different and the volume and urgency of communication varies. If you're a crisis manager, for example, perhaps you need to be checking mail every hour, but only need 5 minutes to respond. You may need to check your email more often, but still make sure you set a boundary. You would schedule 5 minutes an hour in your calendar, and between those times you'd make it a point not to touch your email. For most entrepreneurs, twice a day to deal with messaging is enough. It's important to schedule enough time on a daily basis to handle your typical inbox volume, and to stick to the boundary you set.

My first scheduled time is around 9:30 or 10:00 AM and another one is around 5:00 PM. I don't touch messages between those times unless I've completed everything else I have planned. On a regular day, 30 minutes in the AM and 1 hour in the PM is currently enough to deal with my incoming texts, emails and social media. If you notice the size of your inbox is increasing then increase the time you allocate to spend on it each day.

The second thing to keep in mind around this is to not check text and emails first thing in the morning. Many people roll over in bed when they wake up and the first thing they do is grab their phone. It's one of the worst habits out there and lots of people do it.

There are so many other important things to do first thing in the morning. As part of creating this book, I interviewed some notable entrepreneurs. One thing I notice about these entrepreneurs was that there's a trend in how they start their day. Most begin with gratitude and visualization.

They don't start with finding out who messaged them at 1:00 AM. They don't let someone else's 'emergency' in their inbox mess with their mojo. They start with gratitude, they meditate, work out, spend time with their loved ones and *then* they go to work. They maintain control over their day and how it's going to go and they never turn that power over to anyone else.

When you first implement this habit, people in your life will need to be retrained about it. They'll need time to get used to it. Right now you respond on social media and messaging almost immediately. People have come to expect your responses right away. A sudden change may have them think you're ignoring them or worse that they have annoyed you in some way.

It may take time for the folks in your life to understand that you are no longer available all the time or at their beck and call. You are not sitting waiting for their text message or email 24 hours a day with nothing else to do.

If your business is social media and your job requires you to be connected all day long, that's different. For the rest of us, it's time to take control and be intentional about messaging.

Practice Tips:

- Don't check your phone first thing in the morning for texts and emails.
- Let the people in your life know that you are no longer going to be responding to messages immediately.
- Schedule enough time in your calendar to handle your average quantity of daily messages.
- When your email inbox is grows, schedule more daily time for managing your messages.
- Resist peeking in your inboxes during the day unless you've completed everything scheduled.

Habit #42: Schedule the quantity of time needed to manage your daily inbox volume and stick to the time boundary.

Get Rid of Your To-Do Lists

'For all of the most important things, the timing always sucks. Waiting for a good time to quit your job? The stars will never align and the traffic lights of life will never all be green at the same time. The universe doesn't conspire against you, but it doesn't go out of its way to line up the pins either. Conditions are never perfect. Someday *is a disease that will take your dreams to the grave with you. Pro and con lists are just as bad. If it's important to you and you want to do it* eventually, *just do it and correct course along the way.'*
~ Tim Ferriss, bestselling author of *The 4-Hour Work Week*, entrepreneur, angel investor, and public speaker

This is another one of those contentious habits that entrepreneurs have strong opinions about. Some want to hang on to their to-do lists like a dog with a meaty bone.

A client recently shared with me that she doesn't have a to-do list anymore, and that she got rid of them by accident. She remembers a time not so long ago when she was an 'anal to-do lister,' as she describes it.

When her to-do list would get messy she would create another one and then another one and so on. She wondered if her memory had improved. Then she realized she switched to putting things directly into her calendar over a year ago.

The fundamental thing that most people don't understand about to-do lists, is that lists don't get things done. Everything you do takes a certain amount of time to accomplish. Having a list of 10 things to complete gives me no access to whether everything can and will get done today, or tomorrow, or any day. Maybe only five can get done today and 5 tomorrow. Or only one item will take the entire day. But if I just have a list, I have a bunch of things down with no plan. When you create to-do lists, you avoid having to do the thinking needed to actually plan your life. You end up with long lists of stuff to do with no plan and it creates stress.

Some are so committed to their to-do lists that they are unwilling to consider an alternative. It's not that you necessarily have to give up your to-do lists altogether. It's that on their own, they're incomplete and will not give you access to freedom. I have a list of things that need to get done but I have a different relationship to that list. It's not a 'to-do list' – it's a 'parking lot.' It's where I write everything down that I need to find time in my calendar to schedule. When I have something new to do, either I schedule it right away or it goes to sit in the parking lot.

The moment I schedule it, I delete it from the parking lot. Now it either gets done when I scheduled it or I can move it to some other time to complete it. It no longer needs to be on the parking lot list because it is in my calendar. I follow what my calendar says when it says to do it, and things get done.

Entrepreneurs often say they started their business to be able to do what they want when they want. In other words, they want freedom and flexibility of time. Freedom of time is a completely valid and noble commitment. And, it's unfortunately is not the way your customers are likely willing to relate to you. If you say, 'I will deliver your order when I like,' you will have to work very hard at customer retention.

When you operate from your calendar instead of a list, it allows you to make promises. Then follow what the calendar says you will complete when you said you would complete it. And if for some reason you can't deliver on time, you're able to reschedule and promise a clear, revised time.

If you don't already like putting things in your calendar, this idea may seem daunting. The notion of taking everything from that long list and putting it in your calendar does not seem like a good idea. After all, if you schedule it, then when something changes, doesn't that mean you are going to have to move everything?!

Putting something in your calendar is only half way to having this practice create freedom in your day-to-day. The second part is doing what you said you were going to do when that alarm goes off and says, *Time to…*

Your calendar could say to start the newsletter and instead you choose to work on emails for 30 minutes. Two hours later, you'll need to look for where to find 30 extra minutes to finish the newsletter.

If you need two hours to finish your newsletter, schedule two hours in your calendar. If you start working on it when it says to start, two hours later you have a completed newsletter. You won't need to move anything and now you can move on to the next thing. When I operate this way, I experience little to no stress. I get things done. When there's a large influx of tasks, I may have a short experience of overwhelm. Once it's all in my calendar or the parking lot, I have the experience of freedom again.

My client now operates the same way and there is a new ease that she finds she can manage and take care of her clients with. When she needs to shift things around, she has fewer feelings of guilt. When things were just listed on a piece of paper she would re-write things 6 times because they weren't getting done. Now since using her calendar, the most she has moved things is twice in the last 6 months.

Practice Tips:

- Convert your to-do list into a parking lot. Only put things on the list that you are not yet going to schedule time to complete.
- Schedule time in your calendar for everything you have a promise to complete.
- When you feel overwhelmed with too many things, stop. Schedule everything in your calendar or park items in your parking lot.
- Don't be stubborn about moving beyond your to-do list. You want freedom, don't you?!
- When your calendar says jump, say, 'How high?' halfway up!

Habit #43: Turn all your to-do list items into scheduled items times in your calendar or park them in your parking lot.

Have An Accountability Partner

'Achievement seems to be connected with action. Successful men and women keep moving. They make mistakes but they don't quit.'
~ Conrad Hilton, founder of the *Hilton Hotels* chain

A success partner and an accountability partner are different. A success partner looks with you at specific types of actions you're taking, usually in the Key Area of *Wealth*. They focus on if you're taking actions consistent with meeting your financial goals. A two-way success partner relationship works well and is recommended. Ideally, you and your success partner are both working from weekly promises.

An accountability partner, on the other hand, is someone who coaches you in terms of helping you keep a commitment. Most people do not have a clear understanding of what an accountability partner is. He or she is not someone who tells you what to do. They provide a space to listen to you and to what you say you're committed to.

An accountability partner is someone committed to you achieving the results that you say you want – especially when you don't want to do something or are not doing what's necessary. Accountability partners listen actively in conversations. My best accountability partners are great at asking the right questions.

People think that their accountability partner needs to have skills in the area in which they want to coached. That's not the case. Some of my best accountability partners are not business-oriented at all. And think back to Usain Bolt's Coach, Glen Mills, who we talked about earlier. Coach Mills hasn't a single athletics' medal to his name. Yet that hasn't stopped Usain from getting Olympic Record and World Record breaking results consistently while working with him. The most important thing is that your partner is someone you trust to be brutally honest with you, to hold you to your best standard and to not pull any punches.

There are some common pitfalls in this practice. For one, you can't make your assistant your accountability partner. I've seen entrepreneurs do this. It totally doesn't work – that's someone who could be afraid getting fired. Another poor choice is someone you like having coffee with. Accountability partner interactions are not social activities. Keep your beverage buddies and accountability partners distinct.

Another mistake is thinking that an accountability relationship has to be reciprocal. Just because Bonnie has agreed to be your accountability partner does not mean that you need to be hers. In our experience at *Amorvita*, we've discovered that two-way accountability relationships actually don't work most times.

You can have an accountability partner for any Key Area of Life. When selecting one, look for people who have a higher level of mastery with something than you do. This does not need to be mastery in the area that they agree to be your accountability partner for. Yet it is critical that they have a higher mastery level than you do at *something*. It's important for you to relate them to them as an expert. For example, if is someone is an expert in at finance, they could be your accountability partner for *Well-Being*. Of course, if the person you choose has mastery in *Well-Being* that's a bonus, but it's not necessary.

What *is* necessary is that you have someone who will keep you accountable for what you say you are going to do. They don't help you do the actual planning. You simply hand them your plan and say, 'This is what I am promising. Please hold me accountable.'

I have accountability partners in every major area of my life that I am committed to producing results in. I also have a plan for almost every major area of my life. Sometimes I'm asked if having several accountability partners gets time consuming or becomes a problem. Some of my accountability conversations are only 5 minutes long. My business conversations are typically longer. The trade off of time versus what the conversations provide in my life is completely worth it.

Sometimes when people are first starting a new commitment, they may need more than one accountability person for that one particular area until they become more reliable. The less reliable you are the more support you want to have to keep you accountable. In my Key Area of *Well-Being* I have an endurance coach and a health coach. One works with me on my diet and the other works with me on my training. Having one coach for each of these two aspects of this area is very helpful for me.

Not having accountability partners can be costly. When many of us experience stress, we send it into our bodies and just expect it to get handled on its own. Stress can show up as anything from neck or shoulder tightness to something like cancer. People who have physical well-being issues are often missing accountability partners. The stress of falling behind and breaking promises shows up in their bodies because they are not supported.

Louise Hay is a motivational author who has authored several New Thought self-help books, including the 1984 book, *You Can Heal Your Life*. She describes that the major areas in the body that respond to support or lack of it are the back and bones. When they start to throb or ache, that's all unsupported emotion showing up.[21] People who are unsupported are also usually more irritable. Just take a look in your own experience.

Finally it's always a good idea to test your potential new accountability partners. It's not like you hire them and then you are stuck with them for 6 months. Try them out. It's a good idea to say up front, 'Lets test this out for a couple of weeks or a month and make sure that it works for both of us.'

Having accountability partners will support you in having freedom in your business and in all areas of your life!

---

[21] alchemyofhealing.com/causes-of-symptoms-according-to-louise-hay

Practice Tips:

- Identify what areas you need support in, what you are looking for and what you kind of support you need.
- Have accountability partners for every area of life that you are committed to producing results in.
- Avoid two-way accountability relationships. They rarely work.
- Notice indicators like irritability and aches in the back, neck or knees as signs that you are unsupported.
- Take the necessary actions to get the support you need and find yourself accountability partners who you work well with.

Habit #44: Find an accountability partner in every Key Area of Life you are committed to producing results in.

Stand While You Work

'Posture is nearly connected with the subject of bodily exercise. The usual attitude of a person occupied in reading or writing, tends to obstruct the passage of the blood through the pulmonary and abdominal vessels. Those therefore who are habitually engaged in this manner ought, as much as possible, to stand to their employment. Standing, as it implies muscular exertion, may be regarded as a species of exercise. A valuable treatise might be written on what may be called the diseases of the desk.'
~John Reid, M.D. c.1821

In 2009 a new health catch phrase was born: 'Sitting is the new smoking.' According to a study published in the *Journal of the National Cancer Institute*, sitting for long periods of time increases your risk for cancer. The study found that even in physically active individuals, sitting increased the risk. The risk worsened with each two hour increase in sitting time.[22]

I am blown away by the research on the effects of sitting. I implemented a new practice right away when I heard about this. I now split my time between a kneeling chair, a standing desk and sitting at a table or desk. The desk that my kneeling chair is paired with is not set-up to work at standing up. Rather than having 3 different desks, my plan is to add a variable desk that allows me to work either sitting or standing.

---

[22] theactivetimes.com/ways-sitting-shortening-your-life

A study published in the *American Journal of Epidemiology* found that men and women who sat more than 6 hours a day died earlier than those who limited sitting to 3 hours a day or less. 'Associations were strongest for cardiovascular disease mortality. The time spent sitting was independently associated with total mortality, regardless of physical activity level,' the study found.[22]

What does standing and working have to do with freedom? If you live a longer and healthier life, you get to do more of what you love. Every extra day that I get to fulfill on my vision and passion is a day that I am free.

Sitting also increases the risk of obesity. It's well known that exercise and diet are two major factors in maintaining a healthy weight. According to the Mayo Clinic, the important factor for weight control is moving throughout the day. The clinic conducted a study on weight gain and loss where every aspect of diet and exercise was controlled in a lab. Researchers added 1,000 calories to all the subjects' daily diets. No one was permitted to exercise. Some people were able to maintain their weight while others gained weight. The researchers couldn't understand why some were able to avoid gaining weight without exercise. It turned out, they did so by unintentionally moving more throughout the day.[22]

Understanding the health risks associated with long term sitting is nothing new. The quote at the beginning of this habit is from around 1821, the same year that Mexico declared independence from Spain (that's a fairly long time ago). Hemingway, Dickens and Kirkigard all used standing desks. They were seen as eccentrics because they would work while standing. But the research is clear.

Prolonged sitting also increases the risk of Type 2 Diabetes.[22] In addition, frequent sitters are susceptible to muscular issues. Constant sitting interferes with LPL, an enzyme that breaks down fat and turns it into energy. When the enzyme isn't working as it should, that fat is stored.[22] Sedentary habits are also associated with a higher risk of developing depression.[22]

Prolonged sitting is responsible for as many as 49,000 cases of breast and 43,000 of colon cancer annually in the U.S.[23] Research also found that 37,000 cases of lung cancer, 30,000 cases of prostate cancer, 12,000 cases of endometrial cancer and 1,800 cases of ovarian cancer annually could be related to excessive sitting.[23] That is just crazy!

---

[23] smithsonianmag.com/science-nature/five-health-benefits-standing-desks-180950259

An Australian study done in 2010 found that for every extra hour participants sat daily, their risk of dying increased by 11%.[23] A 2012 study found that if the average American reduced his or her sitting time to three hours per day, life expectancy would climb by two years.[23]

The transition for me from a sitting and kneeling work habit to include standing has been interesting. When I started working standing up, I became aware of muscles that I didn't engage when sitting or kneeling. It was tempting to revert back to what I was comfortable with and it took me a while to get used to. You are likely to need a transition period to adjust from sitting to standing. That's why I love the adjustable desks. They sit on top of your regular desk and you can adjust it as you need to either work sitting down or raise it to work standing up.

Don't let finances or any other excuse stop you from working standing up. I have seen all sorts of interesting setups by entrepreneurs who have committed to doing this. I saw someone use a front door supported on milk crates. Some people work at their breakfast bar in the kitchen and others work at a high-top table in a restaurant. Take control of your well-being and find a way to include standing while you work.

You have the opportunity to enjoy life more, for your body to be is stronger and to not be limited by aches and pains. We are the #1 resource in our business. We need to be healthy. And, as the #1 resource, it's up to us to implement practices that are going to maximize both our health and well-being and that of our team.

Practice Tips:

- Set an alarm to have you stand up from your desk and move around at least once every 30 minutes.
- Allow time for a transition from working mostly in a seated posture to standing. Give your body time to adjust.
- Don't make excuses for why you can't start working standing up immediately. Get creative.
- Invest in a kneeling chair for any seated work that you need to do.
- Introduce standing in your meetings with your team, vendors and clients.

Habit #45: Convert your work environment into a space that supports you and your team standing more.

Take Breaks

'There is virtue in work and there is virtue in rest. Use both and overlook neither.'
~Alan Cohen, businessman, owner of the *Florida Panthers*

I was sharing this habit with a colleague of mine and he got all excited. He said he thinks we have it backward and shared with me he how he learned that.

His first three years in business followed a volume principle. He took as many meetings as he could, attended lots of networking events and crammed more and more into every day. He was certain back then that he knew the path to success.

He shared with me that it was a big surprise to him when he discovered he was wrong. He never took breaks or made time for any rest. He worked 7 days a week. He ate whatever fast food or garbage he could get his hands on while on the run. There were definitely no spaces for meditation or naps planned into his day.

He felt exhausted most of the time and did not produce the results he wanted. Mostly he didn't have the lifestyle he wanted. He justified operating this way because he was pursuing his dreams and had a 'good' life. Or did he? Two years later it caught up with him and he experienced chronic fatigue.

Entrepreneurs mirror this behaviour pattern because of the misconception that working this way will produce the results they want. They don't realize that the longer they go without breaks, the more detrimental to the business they become.

It's not even just that you become less effective; you actually begin to do *detrimental* work. Say you work until 2:00 in the morning without taking any breaks. What you produce is crappy work by your own standards because you're not at your best. Then you put that work out there and that's how you represent yourself. That's detrimental to your business. That's your passion you are messing with.

Seventeen hours awake is equal to a blood alcohol content of 0.05. If your sleepless hours add up to 21, your equivalent blood alcohol content level can reach 0.08. We jail people in many places in the world for driving with that level of alcohol in their system.

Would you board a plane knowing that the pilot has not slept for 17 hours and hasn't taken any breaks? I certainly wouldn't – there's a higher chance of that pilot causing an accident and crashing my flight. Yet on a regular basis, you keep taking big risks that could lead to crashing your business!

After the experience my colleague had of overworking himself, he looked at people like Richard Branson and John Rockefeller and read success blogs. He discovered that something they all have in common is that they take naps. Naps were one of the things that helped him recover when he was sick with chronic fatigue. He now naps often and finds that he often wakes from his nap with new ideas and solutions to problems.

There are different types of breaks. I don't nap on a regular basis. Instead, I meditate in the middle of the day. But the key is I'm in tune with my body and I listen to it. If there's a point in the afternoon that I feel tired and my body is asking for a nap, I take it. I don't ignore it, I don't overpower it and I don't consider it a weakness. I listen.

There are various ways to manage regular breaks during work times. Many people I know are fans of the *Pomodoro Technique* invented by Francesco Cirillo in the late 1980s that we talked about earlier. This technique consists of intervals of uninterrupted periods of 25 minutes and breaks of 5 or 15 minutes. There are free and paid timer apps you can use to manage your Pomodoros. I use one by *TeamViz*.

You will do better work if you structure your day with periods of focused work and breaks in between each. Make sure to give yourself enough time to clear your mind of the last thing you were working on and to begin the next – don't multitask. Multitasking is the opposite of focus. It's very counterproductive compared to taking breaks between periods of focused work.

You may still believe the misguided notion that your brain is designed to multitask. If that's the case, you might be interested in a recent study done by neuroscientists. According to this study, when we attempt to multitask, we don't actually do more than one activity at once. Instead, we actually quickly switch between them. This switching is mentally exhausting. It uses up oxygenated glucose in the brain, running down the same fuel that's needed to focus on a task.[24] 'That switching comes with a biological cost that ends up making us feel tired much more quickly than if we sustain attention on one thing,' says Daniel Levitin, Professor of Behavioral

---

[24] qz.com/722661/neuroscientists-say-multitasking-literally-drains-the-energy-reserves-of-your-brain/

Neuroscience at *McGill University*. Rather than trying to multitask, take breaks between periods of focused activity for the best results.

I manage my breaks a few different ways in my calendar. I have daily time scheduled to meditate and take lunch. I also have an alarm that goes off every 30 minutes to remind me to drink water. When I get up to get that drink, I move around and make sure that I take a mental break for a few minutes. I also always schedule 15 minutes between the items in my calendar. This is so that when something unexpected happens I have room in my schedule to take care of it. When I don't need that extra time, it gives me a chance to have a mental break.

There is no shortage of tips or techniques you can use to inject breaks into your day. The most important thing is to do it. Be mindful of how long you're working at a time. Remember that your brain needs to operate in cycles of concentration and rest.

That colleague of mine is now accomplishing more, has more free time and is actually enjoying his lifestyle, which is why he started his business in the first place. He takes multiple breaks, meditates twice a day and works five days a week. Sometimes he works evenings but when he does he takes long breaks during the day. He's incorporated play into his day as well by doing some kind of playful activity each day. He's happier and getting more and bigger opportunities. He has more time for things that matter like family and his health. He doesn't feel crazy busy all the time. There is momentum in his business and life – and it's a *different* kind of momentum.

Take breaks in your day and see how much more freedom you have as a result!

Practice Tips:

- Set regular alarms to prompt you to get up from your workspace, walk around and give your brain a rest.
- Use a timer to manage your focus time and break times. If you don't already have a timer that works for you, use the *Pomodoro Technique*.
- Stop fooling yourself into thinking multitasking is beneficial for you.
- Identify habits, like multitasking, that have you do work that is detrimental to you, your life and your business and stop doing them.
- Plan times to meditate or nap during your afternoons. Give

yourself the opportunity to come back to your work refreshed.

Habit #46: Schedule regular times to take breaks during your day.

Manage Distractions Effectively

'By prevailing over all obstacles and distractions, one may unfailingly arrive at his chosen goal or destination.'
~ Christopher Columbus, explorer, navigator and colonizer

This habit goes hand in hand with the previous one. Now that you're taking breaks, you want to now maximize your effectiveness and productivity during your focused work periods. The biggest enemy of focus and productivity is the world of distractions.

Gloria Mark, Professor in the Department of Informatics at the *University of California*, Irvine, says that when people are interrupted, it typically takes 23 minutes and 15 seconds for them to return their focus to their work. Most people will do two intervening tasks before going back to their original project. This switching leads to a build up of stress, she says. People with high rates of neuroticism, impulsivity and those susceptible to stress tend to switch tasks more often.[24]

I am such a squirrel chaser (literally, a squirrel running by could distract me). It takes intentional, deliberate strategies and techniques for me to keep my attention focused. I have made a practice of learning from others who use effective methods to manage their focus levels. What do you do to remain focused on what's in front of you instead of chasing squirrels?

I have good friend and fellow squirrel chaser who works in the world of social media. I was interested in finding out what she does to manage her focus. I am fairly certain that if I worked in that industry I would never get anything done. There are constant interruptions. It's one tweet and one post after another. It's like a parade of squirrels.

The first thing she does is she blocks time to work on specific tasks. Secondly, she has rules about her email. She checks it three times a day and then she closes her mail app. Closing the app makes all the difference. There is nothing that is so important that it can't wait two hours. 'Out of sight, out of mind,' she says. During that time, all notifications on her laptop are either closed or turned off.

She trains her clients on what to expect from her with regards to her availability and response time. For anything that is so important that it can't wait 2 hours, her team has other ways to reach her. Her emergency mode of contact is *WhatsApp*. If she sees something from her team or clients on *WhatsApp*, she knows it's time sensitive. For everything else, they don't text, they don't email and they don't bother calling – she never picks up.

She also plans her day out in advance. When it's time for her to community manage (i.e., to manage the different social media feeds for the clients), it's not done in the native apps (directly through the applications). As an agency, that makes sense for her. And the same applies to you as a small business owner running your social media accounts.

Don't community manage in the native app because you'll end up going down the rabbit hole. You respond to a couple of tweets and questions and now the distractions have taken over. The way to get around this is to do all of your managing in apps like *Hootsuite*, *Buffer* and *TweetDeck*. My friend recommends you stay off the native app completely and only log on once a day during scheduled times that you've put in your calendar.

There are generally two reasons entrepreneurs have challenges managing distractions. The first is a lack of planning. Many habits in this book support you in reducing the frequency and quantity of the unexpected. Planning is imperative. Refer back to previous habits and start your planning if you haven't yet.

The second reason is a lack of discipline and respect for yourself. Entrepreneurs react to interruptions. It's like whatever or whoever is interrupting them is more important that what they had planned to do.

In the corporate world, you might actually have to drop something when your manager interrupts you. But you are the CEO of your business. What you say goes. You're the captain of your ship. The distractions and interruptions can get in line until you're ready to deal with them.

Your job as the CEO is to do whatever you need to do to remain focused on what is right in front of you. If you need to close the door, do it. If you need to put your phone on silent, do that. Do you need to install apps to lock you out from certain websites during your working hours? Then that is exactly what there is for you to do.
Recall that Professor Mark said we take over 23 minutes to return to a task

once interrupted. If you break every 30 minutes and allow interruptions, is it any wonder you can never get anything done? You've become a prisoner of your own distractions.

I've gotten much better at controlling my weakness for squirrels. I let my team know at the beginning of every day when I'm available to them and when I'm going to be in focus mode. I limit how many times a day I interact with my messages (Habit #42). I use timers and don't allow myself distractions and interruptions during focus times. When I notice distractions are gaining momentum, I do what I need to do and put in place whatever I need to in order to deal with it right away.

Practice Tips:

- Schedule blocks of time in your calendar to complete specific, focused tasks.
- Turn off or close your phone, notifications and email during focus periods.
- Train your clients, team and vendors on when you're available and when you're not.
- Use apps to support you in remaining focused and keeping 100% of your attention on what you are working on.
- Respect your time. Stop letting yourself get interrupted.

Habit #47: Do whatever you need to do to remain focused on the task at hand that is right in front of you.

Stay Hydrated

'Pure water is the world's first and foremost medicine.'
~ Slovakian Proverb

What does staying hydrated have to do with being an entrepreneur? Was does it have to do with freedom? Well, let's first look at what happens if you don't have an adequate supply of water in your body.

Some of the physical effects of dehydration include:[25]

- A slowdown of enzymatic activity resulting in tiredness and fatigue
- The blood becomes thinker causing resistance to blood flow and causing elevated blood pressure
- Impairing the elimination of toxins through the skin making it more vulnerable to all types of skin disorders
- The production of more cholesterol to prevent water loss from the cells
- Leading to a number of digestive disorders
- The bladder and kidneys being more prone to infection, inflammation and pain
- Waste moving though the intestines more slowly and sometimes not at all, resulting in constipation
- The weakening of cartilage and the slowing of joint repair resulting in pain and discomfort

The effects of being dehydrated are detrimental to your performance. Detrimental performance, as we have discussed many times reduces your ability to create freedom.

These days I'm pretty good, but I used to hate drinking water. I would do just about anything possible to avoid drinking water and I was justified about it. I could frequently be heard saying things like, 'There's water in my juice!' or, '…There's water in my coke!' These days, looking back on that last one makes me chuckle. Who says that!? I would drink calories like you wouldn't believe. There was a point when I consumed less than 8oz of pure water a day. It was likely for me to go an entire day without drinking a drop of water.

I'm amazed at the amount of theories that exist about water consumption. It can be confusing to navigate. I'm going to attempt to simplify it as much as possible here

The first thing to consider is the average human body is 50-65% water. That means that we're more made up of water than anything else. If something makes up more than half your body, would do you want to voluntarily deplete it? When you take away water, you take away a substance that all of your cells need. It is transports the nutrients to your brain. Your organs need it to function. And that's just for starters.

Not drinking enough water is like thinking you can drive your car without

---

[25] getskinnybehappy.com/wp-content/uploads//2013/08/water-health-weight-loss-infographic.jpg

oil. You can run that car with low oil, but you will be doing damage over time. Eventually, the car will just quit. It's the same with your body. You can stay dehydrated for a while, but eventually, your body will stop functioning properly.

Water provides some great health benefits. If you have an interest in losing weight, water ramps up your metabolism and helps you feel full.[26] I swapped my calorie-packed drinks with water. The noticeable effect on my weight was immediate. Drinking a glass of water before meals helps to control hunger. It's a good idea to also look out for empty calories in your drinks (contains added sugars with little to no other nutrition) if you're watching your caloric intake.

About 70-80% of your brain tissue is water. When you're dehydrated both your body and your mind become stressed. By the time you feel thirsty, it's too late because you are already a little dehydrated. Want a quick pick me up in your energy? Drink more water. Want to reduce stress? Keep drinking throughout the day.

Here's another great reason to drink more water: We look better when we're hydrated. Fine lines and wrinkles become deeper when your body is dehydrated. Drinking water hydrates your cells and plumps them up, making you look younger.[27] There's also the added benefit of helping your skin glow by improving circulation and flushing out toxins.[27]

Having enough water in your body also assists with your biological functions. When you're dehydrated your colon becomes dry. This makes it more difficult for you to have proper bowel movements.[27] Dehydration also contributes to a higher incidence of kidney stones. Kidney stones cannot form in diluted urine but crystallize far more easily in the absence of water.[27]

I went to the Mayo clinic website (mayoclinic.org) to find out what they say about how much water we need daily. Here's what they had to say:

> It's a simple question with no easy answers. Studies have produced varying recommendations over the years, but in truth, your water needs depend on many factors, including your health, how active you are and where you live. Although no single formula fits everyone, knowing more about your body's need for fluids will help you estimate how much water to drink each day.[28]

---

[26] webmd.com/diet/news/20040105/drinking-water-may-speed-weight-loss
[27] webmd.com/diet/healthy-water-9/slideshow-water-health
[28] mayoclinic.org/healthy-lifestyle/nutrition-and-healthy-eating/in-depth/water/art-20044256

The Mayo Clinic went on to say that The Institute of Medicine determined that an adequate intake (AI) for men is roughly about 13 cups (3 litres) of total beverages a day. The AI for women is about 9 cups (2.2 litres) of total beverages a day. They pointed out that all fluids counted towards the daily total.[28] You may need to change your total fluid intake depending on how active you are, the climate, your health status and if you're pregnant or breast-feeding.

Interested in some tips to help drink more fluids during the day? Try some of these:

- Stick to a schedule. I have an alarm that goes off every 30 minutes reminding me to have a drink.
- Tie drinking water to something in your routine like meals and snacks.
- Take your water with you. I drink much more water now just because I carry my water bottle with me. It's bright red and occurs like it screams, 'Drink me!'
- Add some fizz or flavour to your water. My brother Dominic adds cucumber or berries to his water because he got tired of drinking it plain. You don't need to spend lots of money on flavoured water when it's so simple to do it naturally.
- Mix it up a little with teas and other healthy beverages.
- Don't forget water rich foods. Soups, salads and watermelon have high water content. And who knew that broccoli is 90% water?!

With a little imagination, you can find many different ways to stay hydrated and healthy.

Of course, it is possible to have too much of a good thing. Over-hydration is called hyponatremia. It's a condition where the level of sodium, an electrolyte that helps regulate water levels in the fluid in and around your cells in your blood, is abnormally low. When this happens, your body's water levels rise and your cells begin to swell. This swelling can cause many health problems, from mild to severe. (add reference)

Do your homework and drink the right amount of fluids every day to remain at your optimum level of hydration.

Practice Tips:

- Understand how much fluid consumption is appropriate for your sex, size and your environment.

- Diversify the ways you get water into your body including through fruits and vegetables.
- Watch out for empty calories in the fluids you consume.
- Try adding fizz or flavour to your water for a little variety.
- Use the colour of your urine as a quick indicator of dehydration. The darker it is, the more dehydrated you are.

Habit #48: Know how much fluid you need to drink each day to stay hydrated and do it!

Be Well Rested

'Much in the way Olympic athletes optimize their game by paying an enormous— borderline maniacal—amount of attention to things like diet, exercise, sleep, and of course the essential R&R, we all would do well to pay more attention to those key aspects of our lives that comprise our overall health equation.'
~ David Agus, physician, *New York Times* bestselling author, Professor of Medicine and Engineering, co-founder of *Navigenics* and *CBS News* contributor

This habit is an extension of Habit #46 where we talked about taking breaks. In this habit we're looking specifically at that one long break called sleep that we take everyday. In this case we're not including naps that you might take during the day as a breaks.

We've already looked at some of the detrimental effects of not getting proper rest. Thank goodness there has been a recent flurry of attention around the sleep crisis that the world is currently experiencing. With any luck, entrepreneurs will finally stop using 4 hours of sleep as a badge of honour. I still know quite a few who do.

Research results impress just how bad a cumulative lack of sleep can be on performance. Subjects in a lab-based sleep study who were allowed to get only 6 hours of sleep a night for 2 weeks straight functioned as poorly as those who were forced to stay awake for 2 days straight. The kicker is, the people who slept 6 hours per night thought they were doing just fine. They rated their own performance as normal even though their cognitive skills where declining.[29]

---

[29] fastcompany.com/3057465/how-to-be-a-success-at-everything/why-six-hours-of-sleep-is-as-bad-as-none-at-all

When I started *Amorvita* I was regularly sleeping 5 to 6 hours a night. I discovered first hand that you really can train your body to operate in a detrimental state. When I was asked about how much sleep I got, I would routinely argue that I only needed 6 hours. As I began doing my sleep research, I discovered that we need 7 to 9 hours according to the National Sleep Foundation.[30] I decided to change this habit for myself. It took me two months to train my body to go from 6 hours to 7 hours of sleep a night. At first I couldn't even stay asleep for 7 hours. I would consistently wake up before my alarm and it took me weeks to learn how to go to bed earlier.

Sleep deprivation can cause damage to your body in the short term. Over time, it can lead to chronic health problems and negatively impact your quality of life:[31]

- Death: Inadequate sleep raises your risk of accidental injury and death from all causes.
- Impaired Brain Activity: Without plenty of rest, your brain is unable to rest and renew, leaving you ill-prepared to face the day.
- Cognitive Dysfunction: When you're sleep deprived, it's hard to concentrate. Your creativity and problem-solving skills deteriorate.
- Memory Problems: Your memory for recent happenings may suffer, and even long-term memories may be difficult to access.
- Moodiness: Sleep deprivation can make you moody, emotional, and quick to anger.
- Hallucinations: If you go long enough without sleep, you may begin to have hallucinations.
- Depression: The long-term effects of sleep deprivation include anxiety, depression, and even thoughts of suicide.
- Micro Sleep: If you are seriously sleep deprived, you might fall asleep for short periods without even knowing it. That can be very dangerous if you're behind the wheel of a car.
- Accident Prone: Lack of sleep can make you groggy and affect your balance and coordination, making you more prone to injury due to accident.
- Weakened Immune Response: Your immune system isn't working at full capacity, so you're more likely to become ill when exposed to bacteria and viruses.
- Weight Gain: Lack of sleep can actually increase your appetite, and your brain may not get the message that you've had enough to eat.

---

[30] cbsnews.com/news/national-sleep-foundation-new-recommendations-for-good-nights-rest
[31] healthline.com/health/sleep-deprivation/effects-on-body

- Type 2 Diabetes: Lack of sleep affects the amount of insulin released after you eat, increasing your risk of developing type 2 diabetes.
- High Blood Pressure: If you have hypertension, a single night without adequate sleep can elevate your blood pressure for a whole day.
- Heart Disease: Sleep deprivation can lead to chronic cardiovascular problems like hypertension and heart disease.

Despite the evidence of the health risks, many entrepreneurs remain proud of working long hours. Something that I have a very hard time with is when coaches and mentors say that this is what it takes for success. Some of those entrepreneurs will soon be lying in a hospital bed with an early life stroke or heart attack. Those same coaching 'professionals' will waltz merrily through life unaware they helped pull the trigger.

You can get your work done and be away from your desk at a decent time. The allowance that you give yourself to work long hours just gives you license to waste time. It's clear that you're not productive when you boast about getting by with little sleep.

A better approach is to focus on being productive. Follow the *Pareto Principle* and do the 20% of the things that make 80% of the difference. Then go to sleep. It's time to end this culture of working all day and night long.

Are you ready to commit to altering your sleep patterns, increasing your productivity and experiencing freedom? If yes, you may need some ideas on how to get started through that process. I know I sure did when I got committed to making a sleep change and even then it took me months to do. Here are some ideas:

- Power down electronics at least an hour before bedtime and cover any display you can't turn off.
- Remove the blue light from electronics as it may interfere with your ability to fall asleep.
- Add apps or select settings on your devices that convert to warmer colours in the evening.
- Don't use warmer colours as an excuse to leave your devices on in that last hour before bed.
- Lower the lights around your home 2 to 3 hours before bedtime.
- Get your neck into a neutral position where it's lined up with the centre of your body when you sleep.

- Increase or reduce the size of your pillow to have your neck aligned properly.
- If you sleep on your back, the pillow should be just large enough to support the curve of your neck.
- Save your bed for sleep and sex only.
- Don't work, surf the internet or watch TV in bed.
- Have your bed and your bedroom be an oasis in your home.
- Keep your pets out of your bed. Their movements can disturb sustained sleep.
- Establish a routine schedule to create your sleep habit.
- Go to bed and wake up at around the same time every morning and evening, even on weekends.

The extent of the difference that extra hour of sleep made to the experience of my life is indescribable. I'm more productive. I do much more than I did before in a shorter period of time. I'm less moody and cranky. Now being short or snappy with someone is on my trigger behaviour list. I'm also more energized and find that I'm more excited about everything in my life.

Start relating to the time you sleep as just as important in your business as the time you're awake.

Practice Tips:

- Look for hidden caffeine in your food and drinks and avoid caffeine as much as possible after 12:00 PM.
- Avoid working out less than 4 hours before your regular bedtime. Exercise creates more energy and is counter-productive to sleep.
- Don't eat big meals or heavy foods too late. Don't eat later then 3 hours before bedtime. Don't drink anything within 2 hours of bedtime.
- Enter your bed with a free mind. Do what you need to do to complete any major decisions, etc. a few hours before bed. Journal before bed to empty your thoughts.
- Reduce environmental noises that could disturb or prevent you from sleeping. Invest in ear-plugs or a white noise generator if necessary.

Habit #49: Do whatever you need to do to get 7 to 9 hours of sleep every night.

Move Your Body

'The critical ingredient is getting off your butt and doing something. It's as simple as that. A lot of people have ideas, but there are few who decide to do something about them, now. Not tomorrow. Not next week. But today. The true entrepreneur is a doer, not a dreamer.'
~ Nolan Bushnell, founder of *Atari, Inc.* and the *Chuck E. Cheese's Pizza-Time Theatres*

This habit is all about doing things regularly that will have you be mobile and active. One of the challenges I often see with entrepreneurs is that they are sedentary a lot of the time. We created a habit that has you stand while you work in Habit #45. It's still important to get up from your work on a regular basis to stretch and move.

My endurance coach, Nat, loves to say, 'We were made to move.' He points out that evolution has given us bodies designed to operate best when they are moving. Embrace the body that you have.

As we've discussed in this book so far, a huge part of freedom is the ability to do as you choose, make choices and explore options. We've discussed that part of the journey is to create the intellectual freedom that we have explored in previous habits. As another part of this journey, you also want to explore freedom *physically* and give yourself the space to embrace movement.

Movement is part of what Nat calls his 'Power Triangle:' Sleep, exercise and nutrition. Exercise is a form of movement. In fact, it's a structured, intense, intentionally stressful, and key part of movement.

I remember really early on in my time working with Nat, I sent him my *Fitbit* weekly summary that showed I had climbed only 11 floors of stairs for the week. I got a reply shortly after saying, 'Dude, do you live on the ground floor? You never increase your altitude. What's up with that?' It was a weak spot that I didn't even notice. That little extra push was all I needed to make my calves do some work. At that time, I was also running on a treadmill with no incline. I pay attention to both of these things now. Yesterday, I was at 42 floors by mid afternoon and was completely surprised. I had done a 40 minute uphill North run and boom – 40-plus floors and I didn't even notice.

In the absence of creating a structure around this habit, we can easily forget to exercise or move about. Before you know it, days pass and you barely move. If you realize you're sitting all day, it's probably time to give yourself a structure.

To start, you could buy a tracker like a *Fitbit* and shoot for 5,000 steps a day for the first month. Or, simply wear it for a month and see how you're doing. Then you'll know what adjustments you have to make to your movement routine.

The next step could be to add at least 2,500 steps a day until you are reliable for moving that much consistently. Then go for 10,000. Once you are reliable for 10,000 see if there's space to shoot for 15,000. You could also make Friday mornings the time you go for a trail ride on a bike, for example.

I love my *Fitbit* because it allows me to play little games with myself. Nat sees people take exercise too seriously. He'll hear people say things like, 'If I can't get on the treadmill or go to the gym, I can't exercise.' Just put on your shoes and go for a walk for 30 minutes and move. If you don't exercise at all at the moment, a 15 or 30 minute walk three times a week for 3 weeks is going to be life changing. When you can add some more, add some more.

Find your baseline and go from there. Our baseline is not what we remember from when we 'were in shape.' It's never about getting back to where you were at some other point in your life or catching up to somewhere you've previously been. Find out where you are at now and improve from there.

I was one of the worst people in the world for this. I was always comparing myself to some past level of performance. I would often go back to myself in my mind as the 25-year-old, martial artist, ripped at 185 lbs. When I would think about being in shape, it was that 25-year-old image of Damian that would come to mind. That was more than two decades ago! I'm not saying it's impossible to get my body into similar shape again. But it would really take something – a lot more than it did when I was that age.

There was a time a few years ago that I didn't exercise at all. Then I started. Recently I realized that I never thought about the guy who 2 years ago started exercising again after not doing so for years. That Damian could only run one minute and walk three minutes before his heart rate hit max. That same guy now goes out and runs for three hours. That's a huge improvement! But I seemed to never think about that. I only compared myself to the me when I was in the best shape of my life. There's no freedom in that. I learned I had to think differently. It was not actually useful for me to be holding myself to that standard. I started setting my measures and celebrating my successes based on where I am *now* and have come from *recently*.

The current shape of your body is a product of your past, not your present. If you have a fit body and in the last few weeks you turned into a couch potato, your body might still appear fit right now, but changes will show in time. The same is true if you are out of shape and currently in a committed exercise program. What you see on the outside is a reflection of all of the time you spent less active. Give yourself credit for all the good work you are doing now.

It's self-deprecating and counterproductive when we don't recognize and celebrate our accomplishments. Many of us reach a milestone or target and then move on to the next thing with no second thought. Taking time to celebrate is important. You will find freedom in celebrating your accomplishments and always looking at how far you've come.

In this world of exercise and getting moving you can always achieve new personal bests. You can do more reps, do something in less time, lift more weight, etc. Push yourself to keep improving in this area but also learn to celebrate your wins. Then take those wins into other parts of your life.

Your first win could just be to start adding some more movement into your day for a few minutes at a time. If you're feeling time crunched, and you know you're committed to getting moving, try these 10 exercises that you can do from your desk:[32]

- Paper Push-ups – With both hands on your desk, walk your feet back until your legs are at a 45-degree angle. Do a dozen push-ups from that position.
- Book Press – Grab the heaviest book you have. Hold it behind your head, then extend your arms up. Drop it back down to your neck and repeat.
- Shoulder Blade Squeezes – Pretend to hold a pencil between your shoulder blades and squeeze them together for 10 seconds. Release, the repeat.
- Office Yoga – Keep a mat curled up under your desk and whip it out for instant Zen.
- Chair Squats – Standing six inches in front of your chair, lower

---

[32] time.com/4019563/exercise-work-desk

yourself down until your butt hits the edge of the chair. Then pop back up.

- Triceps Desk Dips – Facing away from your desk, place hands shoulder width apart with legs extended. Bend your arms. Then mostly straighten to keep tension on your triceps and off your elbow joints.
- Wall Sits – Stand against a blank wall space, then squat down to a 90 degree angle. Slide back up and repeat.
- Standing Calf Raises – Starting with your feet together, rise up to raise your calves. Hold for 10 seconds, release and repeat.
- Get a (Leg) Raise – While sitting, straighten your leg and hold for 10 seconds. Lower it almost to the floor, hold, and repeat on the other side.
- Phone Pacing – Get a headset so every time your phone rings, you can pace while talking.

Get your body moving. You'll find freedom in moving your body in new ways, freedom in pushing yourself to do more exercise, and in freedom in celebrating your accomplishments!

Practice Tips:

- Take credit for all of the good work you are doing now and stop being hard on yourself for what you did or didn't do in the past.
- Stop comparing yourself now to who or where you used to be.
- Move your body during your work day. Find creative ways to include movement in your day.
- Own a movement tracker like a *Fitbit* or similar device. Play progressive games to increase the amount of movement in your days and weeks.
- Get outside as often as possible during your day.

Habit #50: Get your body moving for at least 150 minutes a week.

Make Wise Food Choices

'The way you think, the way you behave [and] the way you eat can influence your life by 30 to 50 years.'
~ Deepak Chopra, author, public speaker and alternative medicine advocate

There are all sorts of ways you could approach this particular habit. Some people follow 'eating right for their blood type.' There are paleo diets, macrobiotic diets and much more. I don't care what system or structure you chose. What matters is that you choose a system or structure. That tells me you are already headed in the right direction. That's what I care about.

Food is the fuel for your body. You need to make wise food choices if you want your body to run well. You are already aware that fast foods and junk are not good for sustaining the body of an entrepreneur. I'm not going to attempt to tell you what to eat; especially not in the space allocated here. There are many books and experts you can consult for advice on this. Again, the important thing is that you find what's right for you and that you have a plan in the first place.

When I started *Amorvita*, I was eating relatively well. At the time, I was in a relationship with someone who was gluten-free and ate little dairy. There were lots of green leafy foods in my diet.

When that relationship ended, I started operating from the opposite end of the spectrum. Grocery shopping consisted of food that was easy to prepare or reheat. My neighbourhood fast food chains recognized my favourite orders.

The unhealthy eating combined with no exercise (yes I stopped that too) led to me being the heaviest weight I'd ever been in my life. I felt fat and embarrassed about my physical appearance. How could I be talking about living the life of a thriving entrepreneur in all 12 Key Areas of Life and look like that?

If you don't take care of your body you're harming your business. We've already looked at what happens when you do detrimental work when your body is in an impaired state. Sabotaging your fuel source is another way to reduce your business' opportunity for success.

To achieve the kind of freedom you want in your life, you will need to be operating as effectively as possible. I always relate to the body of an entrepreneur to a high-performance machine, like a *Formula One* race car. Imagine what would happen to that car's performance if you filled it with regular fuel – not much chance of winning a race.

As we've already discussed in several other habits, one of the biggest challenges entrepreneurs seem to face is a busy schedule. That's the case for this habit as well. 'Not having enough time' appears to contribute to poor eating habits.[33] When you're in a time crunch, it's easy to start skipping meals, consuming too much caffeine, sugar, frozen and junk foods, multi-tasking while eating and eating too much. Each of these behaviours comes with its own set of detrimental effects on the body.

Skipping breakfast and other meals deprive the body of the nutrients and energy needed to fuel you. When your body is not properly fed, your brain cannot work at maximum capacity. You become detrimental to your business. You may also experience other symptoms including fatigue, dizziness and even aggressiveness.[34] I get 'hangry,' irritated and have a short fuse in the absence of food or when my blood sugar is low.

Too much caffeine can lead to a variety of health issues. At the lower end of the spectrum, it can cause heartburn, restlessness and dehydration. At the other end of the spectrum, it can cause ulcers, cardiac issues and comas.[35] Too much sugar will never help you be more productive. You will ride the up and down swing of the sugar highs and lows and turn those calories into unwanted fat. Frozen, fast and junk foods put the wrong types of substances in your body that negatively impact your ability to focus and therefore your productivity.

There are simple things you can do to make wiser food choices and develop healthier eating habits:

- Get into the habit of planning your meals in advance.
- Create a menu for the week for some or all your meals.
- Watch for times in your calendar where you may be crunched for time and tempted to go with a fast food option. Plan something else instead, like leaving extra room in your day to pack a lunch or snack.
- Resist the temptation and quick fix of skipping a meal, especially breakfast.
- Plan to get up 30 minutes earlier and go to bed 30 minutes sooner to create time in your calendar for a proper breakfast.
- Solve the challenge of time to prepare breakfast by having protein shakes or smoothies.
- Keep healthy snacks at home and with you for those unexpected situations where time is scarce.

I tend not to be an all-or-nothing type of person. So what about those times

---

[33] everydayhealth.com/diet-and-nutrition-pictures/bad-eating-habits-and-how-to-break-them.aspx#05
[34] entrepreneurs-journey.com/1444/7-eating-habits-that-sabotage-your-productivity-as-an-entrepreneur
[35] inc.com/sarah-kimmorley/19-horrible-things-that-can-happen-if-you-drink-too-much-caffeine.html

that you crave something delicious that is also unhealthy? I say, why not have a taste? It's great to treat yourself. But only have a little bit! One of my colleagues loves getting those little containers of *Haagen Daz* ice cream. It may only be a few teaspoons but she gets a taste and it handles her craving.

After getting fed-up with the condition of my body, I hired a macrobiotic health coach to work with me on food. When I interviewed her she said something that made a huge difference. She made me realize that if I could alter the quality of my blood, then I could alter the function of every cell in my body. I could improve my brain function and change my moods. Not to mention I could gain energy to call upon to create the life of freedom I'm committed to.

Learning to eat mostly macrobiotic (remember: I'm not all or nothing!) was interesting. I grew up with meat as a part of every meal. The notion of eating only deep sea, white fish as my only animal protein was shocking. I learned new information about different ways I could consume protein from alternate sources.

I still don't think tofu is a real food, but I have a whole new appreciation and love for organics and vegetables. The most important thing I noticed as I went through this transition was that I became conscious of my food choices. Now, when I eat something outside the macrobiotic world, it's intentional. And I'm aware of the effect that all of the food I eat it has on my body, productivity and life.

Practice Tips:

- Plan your meals in advance. Cook on your scheduled days off for the rest of the week or hire someone to cook for you.
- Pack your lunch with healthy, nutritious foods to eat when you're working away from home.
- Don't skip meals, especially breakfast. Keep healthy snacks with you for emergencies.
- When you have a food craving, treat yourself with a small taste of it. Discipline yourself.
- Reduce and then eliminate the unholy five - caffeine, sugar, frozen, fast and junk foods.

Habit #51: If you wouldn't feed it to an Olympic athlete before a gold medal event, stop eating it.

Protect Your #1 Resource

'When everything seems to be going against you, remember that the airplane takes off against the wind, not with it.'
~ Henry Ford, founder of the *Ford Motor Company*

My foundational principle is: You are the #1 resource for your business. If you don't work then your business doesn't work. Entrepreneurs often lose sight of this from a holistic perspective. I understand you will figuratively bleed for your business and give everything you can. But understand that there are costs and trade offs with every choice that leads to a poor entrepreneurial habit.

There is a trade-off to not eating well. There is a trade-off to not sleeping well. There is a trade-off to not drinking enough water. There is a trade-off to not exercising. There is a trade-off to working until 10 o'clock every night. There are trade-offs to all of the choices you make. For each habit in this book, the choices you make are either leading you closer to freedom or further away from it. There are no neutral actions.

The sum of poor habit choices has the #1 resource for your business be less effective. Entrepreneurs seem to have a very hard time seeing and remembering this. They start to feel sick and they push themselves harder to work through it. Having my clients take care of the most important resource first is an ongoing challenge.

Think about separating the business as one entity and yourself as another. Now imagine your business was evaluating you doing business with a customer. Would you allow that customer to drain your business? Customer exchanges need to help the business and vice versa. If the business drains you, that's a bad deal. You should go do something else that adds to your life in positive ways.

Entrepreneurs often think, I'll let the business drain me for a while because I've invested a lot. The justification is that at some point it's going to explode, make tons of money and that then it will all have been worth it. That idea or way of thinking has limited viability. As we have seen in the previous 51 habits it does not take much to start operating detrimental to your business. Detrimental performance will never equal sustainable success.

The same is true with managing customer relationships in your business. If you start a client relationship on grounds that don't work, it drains the business. There has to be workability, an effective, practical or feasible relationship. You could start a new client relationship and charge them less than it costs you to provide the product or service. That has no workability. You might eventually charge higher rates but you still started on unequal ground with a lack of respect. You start off with something you will grow to resent. That's another bad deal.

The same principle applies to your life at large. Don't make a bad deal. We have no statistical evidence for bad deals actually ending up successful down the road or paying back later. In fact, evidence is there for the opposite. 96% of businesses fail within 10 years according to Inc.[36]

The statistical evidence for failed businesses is astronomical. It's so high that you could make the argument that the entrepreneurial system is broken. It's fair to say that a high portion of this percentage comes from the way entrepreneurs run their lives and the choices they make. Don't let yourself get stuck with bad deals.

It's so easy to slip into a mindset that has us make bad deals. Sometimes the bad deals are with ourselves. I did this when I first started writing this book. Faced with an editing deadline for my first draft, I made the short term deal to put *all* my time into writing. Over the course of two and a half weeks, my sleep dropped to an average of 5.5 hours per night including some nights with no sleep at all. I skipped meals, ate fast food and skipped workouts.

It only took about a week for my body to start sending signals that it had had enough. I'm grateful for all of the work I've done to notice the signs that in the past I would have missed or ignored. Despite all the warnings I kept going in a detrimental state. Finally, at the end of two and half weeks, my body really had had enough and I had to take three full days off. It's amazing that I used to operate that way on a regular basis and that so many of my colleagues continue to do so. I took the time off and celebrated how far I've come in setting healthy habits as an entrepreneur, knowing when I deviate from them, and knowing how to get myself back on track.

I don't believe businesses fail because entrepreneurs don't know what they're doing. I also don't think they fail because it's inevitable or has to be that way. I think entrepreneurs fail because they're not set up to win, *holistically*. People know what they're doing in terms of the services they provide to their customers. What they need help with is knowing what to do to run a business *that keeps them healthy while providing those services*.

---

[36] inc.com/bill-carmody/why-96-of-businesses-fail-within-10-years.html

I don't want to see entrepreneurs get coaching and advice that tells them to do the opposite anymore. Bad advice makes them take their #1 resource and strip it down and run until the battery is done. It simply doesn't work. It doesn't provide freedom for the courageous business owners who give it all to their dreams. Sure, a few might make it operating this way, but the greater percentage of businesses heading in this direction will fail. And even worse, the entrepreneurs will fail to actually live, in reality, the freedom they seek.

Using the equilibrium-based, holistic approach to live life as an entrepreneur that you've learned in this book will not necessarily grow your business the fastest. But it *is* the pathway for growing a *healthy* business that will thrive *sustainably*. It's the pathway that enables success and freedom. You can have a healthy relationship with the business and with yourself inside and outside of your business. And you can also have healthy relationships with all of the things that are important to you. These 52 habits are the pathway to support you in achieving freedom – the freedom you told yourself you wanted when you started your entrepreneurial journey.

Your first job is to make sure you're in a great place so that you can give the business what it needs. Of all of the areas in the *Entrepreneurs 12 Key Areas of Life*, *Business* is the foundation. Having a business that thrives provides access to resources like time, money and a team.

The other 11 Key Areas of Life provide the support to have *you and* your business thrive. It is an interrelated system that needs all of the parts working at equal levels. Your physical body cannot function at its best level when one of its systems isn't working. Likewise, an entrepreneur does not function at an optimal level when the 12 Key Areas of Life are not in a state of equilibrium with each other. Your most important job as an entrepreneur is to protect the #1 resource in your business…*YOU!*

Practice Tips:

- Notice where you're willing to trade in yourself for the business. Don't make bad deals.
- Listen to your body. When it asks for rest or time off, take it.
- Don't work when you're sick. Give yourself time to recover and heal.
- Stop accepting any coaching or advice that has you put your business before yourself.
- Focus on the freedom you deserve in the choices you make in life.

Habit #52: Take whatever steps are necessary on a minute by minute and day by day basis to protect your #1 resource... *YOU*!

THE 52 HABITS

Habit #1: Spend intentional time with business owners who live their dreams and operate the way you aspire to.

Habit #2: Attend at least four group networking events and four one-on-ones per month.

Habit #3: Choose an expert coach for every area of your life in which you want to produce extraordinary results.

Habit #4: Take part in at least one immersive personal growth activity per quarter.

Habit #5: Create a trigger behaviour checklist and review it at least once weekly.

Habit #6: Schedule time to spend with yourself and your thoughts…get to know the person within.

Habit #7: Read or listen to something industry related every day.

Habit #8: Become an expert with your marketing and sales math for everything you sell.

Habit #9: Schedule your non-negotiables in your calendar then manage your life with the time remaining.

Habit #10: Create and design your work environment to match the results you are committed to producing.

Habit #11: Identify the tasks you hate and give them to someone who loves doing them.

Habit #12: List all of the tasks you do that you are not great at and plan to delegate them all with specific deadlines.

Habit #13: Identify your favourite time suckers and either get rid of them or schedule (and stick to!) appropriate times for them.

Habit #14: Document, map and operate your business using workflow processes.

Habit #15: Know what matters to your team and check in with each person daily.

Habit #16: Create and develop powerful, real relationships with everyone you interact with.

Habit #17: Get very clear on your *Why*. Share it and be completely unshakeable about it.

Habit #18: Create a powerful, inspiring 10-year vision that includes all 12 Key Areas of Life.

Habit #19: Create your vision board and intentionally connect to it emotionally daily.

Habit #20: Create your bucket list and the plan to accomplish 3-5 items per year.

Habit #21: Create and maintain your 5-, 3- and 1-year life plans.

Habit #22: Connect people. Support others in fulfilling their aspirations and dreams on a daily basis.

Habit #23: Practice gratitude daily and often.

Habit #24: Fiercely protect your sacred messages and new ideas like a mother bear protects her cubs.

Habit #25: Create, nurture and cherish a strong, powerful partnership with a romantic partner.

Habit #26: Set aside regular weekly time to nurture your important friendships and social relationships.

Habit #27: Have a regular spiritual practice that provides a space for you to be grounded.

Habit #28: Do something every day that contributes positively to your state of well-being.

Habit #29: Take actions to alter your self-talk when you start conversations to diminish your greatness.

Habit #30: Refuse to tolerate environments that do not deliver spaces of freedom and creativity. Stop and make immediate changes.

Habit #31: Schedule a weekly time to identify any family relationships that have something 'off.' Take immediate action to get whatever it is resolved.

Habit #32: Make a list of 50 things that make you happy and do at least one of them every week.

Habit #33: Practice a routine of daily and weekly growth activities that you consider non-negotiable.

Habit #34: Every morning ask yourself, who will you contribute to today and how will you contribute to life?

Habit #35: Identify where you are surviving your business and take immediate actions to create freedom.

Habit #36: Identify everything that lacks integrity in the area of *Wealth* and begin resolving each.

Habit #37: Set-up, create and visualize your day before you go to sleep the night before.

Habit #38: Schedule time during in the last week of each quarter to create quarterly and weekly promises.

Habit #39: Establish a daily cut-off time and honour it.

Habit #40: Take two full days off per week and at least one full week off per quarter.

Habit #41: Schedule a creative day each week and go somewhere inspiring.

Habit #42: Schedule the quantity of time needed to manage your daily inbox volume and stick to the time boundary.

Habit #43: Turn all your to-do list items into scheduled items times in your calendar or park them in your parking lot.

Habit #44: Find an accountability partner for every Key Area of Life you are committed to producing results in.

Habit #45: Convert your work environment into a space that supports you and your team standing more.

Habit #46: Schedule regular times to take breaks during your day.

Habit #47: Do whatever you need to do to remain focused on the task at hand that is right in front of you.

Habit #48: Know how much fluid you need to drink each day to stay hydrated and do it!

Habit #49: Do whatever you need to do to get 7 to 9 hours of sleep every night.

Habit #50: Get your body moving for at least 150 minutes a week.

Habit #51: If you wouldn't feed it to an Olympic athlete before a gold medal event, stop eating it.

Habit #52: Take whatever steps are necessary on a minute by minute and day by day basis to protect your #1 resource…YOU!

ABOUT THE AUTHOR

Damian Reid is the Founder and CEO of *Amorvita Inc.*, based in Toronto, Canada. He is an international speaker, author and entrepreneur expert.

Damian has led many advanced leadership and personal development programs. He has helped clients make significant, positive changes in their professional and personal lives. He believes in making a difference by helping people pursue their passions and create the life they love. Damian's greatest passion is making a real difference with entrepreneurs, who he believes are the most courageous people on the planet.

Clients find him when they want to accomplish the FREEDOM they started their businesses to experience. They want to work fewer hours and claim more time off while radically increasing their bottom-line. Many want more vitality and time to spend on the important things that really matter in their lives including family, recreation and spiritual pursuits.

Damian founded *Amorvita Inc.* in 2013. Its international network of coaches, service providers and specialists provide business owners with real solutions and pathways to the FREEDOM they desire. His team is committed to existing as a globally recognized voice transforming the way one million entrepreneurs live and work!

At 13 years old, Damian started his first successful company doing what he loved from his mother's basement. In addition to 20 years in senior management roles for major telecommunications companies, ad agencies and personal training and development companies, 15 years of experience is in running six of his own businesses. Media appearances include Canada AM (CTV), Small Business TV (CTV), Cityline (City TV), The Nature of Things (CBC), Toronto Living (Rogers 10), 640 AM, British Airways in-flight, Chatelaine, Pursuit, MENZ, Canadian Press, Toronto Star, Toronto Sun, and National Post.

When not working you can find him knocking the latest items off his Top 100 "Bucket" List…16 complete. He's currently working on learning Spanish, running his 1st marathon and mastering Salsa dancing.

QUICK ORDER FORM

Satisfaction guaranteed

✒ **Email Orders**: info@entrepreneurialitis.com

☏ **Telephone Orders**: Call 1-416-574-8080

Please have your credit card information ready.

🖃 **Postal Orders**: Send this form to FREEDOM Publishing, a division of Amorvita Inc., 1 Scott Street, Suite 706, Toronto, Ontario M5E 1A1.

Please send me the following quantity of books _____. I understand that I may return any of them for a full refund for any reason, no questions asked.

See Amorvita's web site (amorvita.ca) for FREE information on: other books, speaking/seminars, programs, mailing lists, coaching.

Name:

Address:

City, State/Province, Postal Code:

Telephone:

Email:

Credit Card #:

Name on card:

Expiry Date, CVV: